SCOTTISH
SURNAMES

SCOTTISH
SURNAMES

George Mackay

Lomond

Cover photograph reproduced with permission from the George
Washington Wilson Collection, Aberdeen University Library

© 1998 Waverley Books Ltd
David Dale House
New Lanark ML11 9DJ

ISBN 0 947782 38 9

Printed and bound by Mackays of Chatham

2 4 6 8 10 9 7 5 3 1

Introduction

The many and varied surnames in use in Scotland come from three main language sources. The largest is the Gaelic language and its cultural tradition. This harks back to the time when Scotland was a predominantly Gaelic-speaking country, with Scots (a form of Northumbrian English) common only in the southeast. Many Scots-sounding names are actually 'scotticised' Gaelic, and others are translations of names originally Gaelic, but the Scots language itself is also a source of many names. The third great source is Scandinavia. In the early Middle Ages, vast areas of northern and western Scotland were ruled by Norway. The Viking legacy is still apparent in the names found in those parts of the country. Indeed, the local distribution of certain names remains a striking feature throughout the country, especially in its northern and southwestern extremities, showing the tenacity and durability of farming families and fishing communities.

There are others sources too. The political alliance with France brought French names and styles, like Stuart. Trading contact with the Low Countries brought in Dutch names. Immigrants acquired names like Inglis and Fleming.

How did surnames arise? To condense a lengthy and complicated social process, it might be put like this. When Scotland had a population of fewer than a million spread fairly evenly throughout the country, all communities were very small (Edinburgh far the largest with about 10,000 people). Everyone had a baptismal name. For males, the most common name was John (Gaelic Iain) and the range of names was not vast. To distinguish between the many Johns and Joans, nicknames arose – John Red-Head, Joan Left-handed. A priest might take the name of his patron saint, as in Gilmartin. As the political organisation of the country grew and communities became more aware of their own identity and of their interaction with others, the group name became important. With the Celtic clan system (*clann* means 'children'), the identity of the local group was very often expressed in the common name that made them all the children of a remote ancestor, as with the Robertsons, Clan Donnachie (children of Duncan). This name showed a man's affiliation: a vital piece of information in the tribal society.

The majority of Scottish surnames are patronymics – fathers' names – or location names from the place where the original bearer lived.

The organisation of social life was changed in the twelfth and thirteenth centuries by the arrival of Norman-French knights who were given grants of land by the kings. The Celtic tribal system was not for them; they set up markets and small towns, and saw the people more as peasantry than as clansfolk. There was an urge to classify everyone, made all the stronger by the expectation that a son would follow his father's trade or occupation. John the Hunter or John the Baker (Baxter) would be succeeded by another John the Hunter or John the Baker. But sometimes the father would become John the Old and the son John the Young.

All the efforts of lairds and barons could not prevent a certain social mobility. If John the Baker left his burgh of Dingwall to live elsewhere, he might be known there as John the Stranger or John of Dingwall, and his family would take the same surname. Names afforded protection. When the Lyon family dominated Strathmore, many Angus hill dwellers changed their names to Lyon and gave allegiance to the head of that clan, seeking safety in numbers. Names also could be deadly. When the MacGregor name was banned in the sixteenth century under pressure from the Argyll Campbells, its use was punishable by death. Many MacGregors, ironically, assumed the name of Campbell (under the friendlier Campbell of Breadalbane).

Some names denoted a clan's territory, like Ross in both the north and southwest.

Social convention and necessity meant that almost everyone had a surname by the fourteenth century. And social mobility meant that the name often no longer described the trade or affiliation of its bearer. A Miller might be a fisherman; a Caird might be a wealthy settled merchant; a Smith a professor of philosophy.

Names remain fluid. Despite the hundreds of surnames listed in this book, it is not a complete list. It includes names that are exclusively Scottish and names that are common in other parts of the British Isles as well but have a strong and well-established Scottish presence. Smith is one of the most frequently found surnames in Scotland as it is in England. In the nineteenth century, many thousands of Irish immigrants brought their own Celtic names into Scotland, and Irish names are numerous in central Scotland. This book does not set out to include these, although a hard-and-fast rule would be impossible to keep. This applies particularly to names that have crossed the North Channel more than once in both directions from Argyll and Galloway to northeast Ireland.

A

Abercrombie, Abercromby
Location name from mouth of the River Crombie in Fife. Sir Ralph Abercromby (1734–1801) was a distinguished general in the Napoleonic wars.

Abernethy
Location name from the town (mouth of the River Nethy), Perthshire.

Acheson *see* Aitchison.

Adams, Adamson
Patronymic: son of Adam. James and Robert Adam (1730–94, 1728–92) were the leading architects and interior designers of their time. *See also* Eadie.

Addie, Addy *see* Eadie.

Affleck
Form of Auchinleck; one who lives at the place of flagstones.

Agnew
From the Norman French location name d'Agneaux, 'place of the lambs'; the family established itself at Lochnaw in Wigtownshire in the thirteenth century.

Ainslie
From Old English, 'Aene's meadow', a Lothian and Border name.

Aird
From Gaelic *ard*, 'ridge'; 'dweller on the hill'.

Airlie
A form of Arrol.

Aitchison
A southern Scottish form of Atkinson (*see also* Aitken). In the Borders, the name was formerly Atzin, with the z pronounced as y, and Aitchison derives from that. Also spelt Acheson.

Aitken
Scots form of Atkin ('little Adam' or 'little Arthur'). Also Atkinson, 'son of Atkin'.

Aitkenhead
Location name from Lanarkshire, first recorded in the late thirteenth century. Probably Aitken is from Scots *aiken*, 'oaken'.

Albany
May be from Gaelic Albannach, 'a Scot'; or old French Aubigny; or Latin *albanus*, 'white'.

Alexander
From Greek, meaning 'defender of man', but the name is a tribute to the fame of Alexander the Great. More common in the west and south (there was an Alexander sept of Clan Donald) and can also be an English version of MacAlister.

Allan
Mostly found in the northeast, although the Allan river is in Perthshire. From Gaelic *ailinn*, 'rock'. Also spelt Allen.

Allardyce
Location name from Kincardineshire. The Gaelic elements mean 'south cliff'.

Allen *see* Allan.

Alloway
Location name from Ayrshire, birthplace of Robert Burns, but can also be from Alloa, Clackmannanshire. From Gaelic *al a' mhaigh*, 'rock in the plain'.

Almond
Location name from River Almond (Midlothian and Perthshire), from Gaelic *amhainn*, 'river'.

Alpin
A Pictish name, its derivations are uncertain. *See also* MacAlpin.

Anderson
Patronymic: 'son of Andrew' (from Greek, 'manly'). As Andrew was patron saint of Scotland, it may also have been a more general descriptive name for a Scot. James Anderson (1739–1808) was a pioneer in new agricultural methods.

Andrew, Andrews
Patronymic: 'son of Andrew'.

Angus
From Gaelic *aon*, 'one', and *gus*, 'strength'; 'uniquely strong'. The county name is from an eighth-century Pictish King Angus.

Annand
Location name from Annan, Dumfriesshire, but now found mostly in Aberdeenshire.

Anstruther
Location name from the town in Fife from Gaelic *an sruthair*, 'the stream'.

Arbuthnot, Arbuthnott
Location name from Kincardineshire from Gaelic *aber baothonaich*, 'the fool's marsh'. Dr John Arbuthnot (1667–1735) was the addressee of Swift's 'Epistle to Dr Arbuthnot'.

Archibald
Of German origin, meaning 'precious-bold', it was used as a surname in Scotland to indicate a monk through a misunderstanding of the -bald. *See* Gillespie.

Argo
A localised name from Aberdeenshire.

Armour
Maker of armour. The maiden name of Robert Burns's wife, Jean.

Armstrong
From Old English, meaning 'strong-armed'. The name of a famous family of the Borders, especially Liddesdale, lairds and raiders, the most famous or notorious being Johnnie Armstrong (died 1530). William Armstrong (sixteenth century) is the 'Kinmont Willie' of the Border ballad.

Arnot, Arnott
Location name from Kinross-shire, perhaps from Old English *earn*, 'eagle'.

Arrol
Location name from Errol, Perthshire. Sir William Arrol (1839–1913), born in Houston, Renfrewshire, built the second Tay Bridge and collaborated on the Forth Bridge.

Arthur
From old Gaelic *art*, 'bear': giving Artair, 'bear-like', a personal name.

Atholl
Location name from the district in Perthshire (Gaelic, 'ford of Fotla').

Atkinson *see* Aitken.

Auchterlonie, Auchterlonie
Location name from near Forfar, from the thirteenth century.

Auld from Scots *old*. *See* Oag.

Ayton, Aytoun
Location name from Berwickshire: town on the river Eye. W. E. Aytoun (1818–65) was a popular versifier of the nineteenth century who wrote *Lays of the Scottish Cavaliers*.

B

Baikie
Location name from Angus and also found in Orkney.

Baillie
From French *bailli*, Scots *bailie*: 'steward' or 'official'. John Baillie (1886–1960), born in Gairloch, was a leading theologian; Dame Isobel Baillie (1895–1983) was a celebrated singer of oratorios such as Handel's 'Messiah'.

Bain
From Gaelic *ban*, 'white' or 'pale', a descriptive name. Also spelt Bayne.

Baird
From Gaelic *bard*, 'minstrel'. Most commonly found in Ayrshire. John Logie Baird (1888–1946) was the pioneer of television.

Balfour
Location name from Fife, possibly Gaelic-Pictish 'pasture-place'. Sir Andrew Balfour (1630–94) established a physic garden in Edinburgh in 1676. Arthur Balfour (1848–1930) was prime minister of the UK.

Ball
From Celtic *bal*, 'a spot'. A descriptive name or nickname.

Ballantyne, Bannatyne
Location name from numerous areas. The Gaelic elements mean 'place of the farmstead'. R. M. Ballantyne (1825–94) wrote *Coral Island* and many other adventure stories.

Balliol
Norman-French *bailleul*, 'the fortified place'. Name of the ill-starred King John of Scotland who reigned 1292–96.

Banks
'Dweller on the river bank'.

Bannerman
'Standard-bearer'; perhaps also 'standard-maker'. But the first recorded Bannerman was the king's doctor (1368).

Barbour
Scots *barber*. John Barbour (*c*.1316–96) wrote the epic poem *The Brus* on the exploits of King Robert I.

Barclay
An Aberdeenshire name but originally from Berkeley in England. The banking family came from Montrose. Captain Barclay-Allardice of Urie (1779–1854) was a famous long-distance walker.

Barnet, Barnetson
Form of the name Bernard, made popular in the Middle Ages by St Bernard of Clairvaux. Barnieson, a Caithness name, is also a form of it.

Barns
Old English and Scots, 'dweller by the barn'. Also spelt Barnes.

Barr
From Gaelic *barr*, 'hilltop': 'dweller on the heights'. A location name from Ayrshire and Renfrewshire.

Barrie
A form of Barr. Also a location name from Angus ('place of the burial mounds'). The author of *Peter Pan*, J. M. Barrie (1860–1937), came from Kirriemuir in Angus.

Barron
From Gaelic *baruinn*, 'a small landowner' or 'bonnet laird'. A name from Inverness and Aberdeen.

Baxter
Scots, 'baker'. A craft name. Stanley Baxter was a well-loved actor and performer.

Bayne *see* **Bain.**

Beaton
From Latin *beatus*, 'blessed', through Old French (i.e. 'faithful believer'); alternatively, 'dweller by the beehives'. This name also acquired a French form as Bethune during the period of the Auld Alliance. Cardinal David Beaton (1494–1546) was chancellor of Scotland.

Beattie
From Gaelic *biadhtaiche*, 'supplier of food'; the clan chief's victualler for guests. Also from Bate, Baty, shortened forms of Bartholomew.

Beedie
A form of Beattie, found mostly in Aberdeenshire.

Begbie
From Old Norse, 'dweller at Begga's farm or homestead'. A Lothian name.

Begg
Descriptive name from Gaelic *beag*, 'small', 'a small person'.

Begley
From Gaelic *beag*, 'small', and *liath*, 'grey'. 'Little grey man'.

Beith
Location name from the Ayrshire town, from Gaelic *beith*, 'birch'. The novelist Ian Hay (1876–1952), was actually named John Hay Beith.

Bell
Found throughout Scotland, it has several sources: Old French *bel*, 'handsome' – a nickname; Old English *belle*, 'a bell' – a craft name for a bell-ringer or maker. It is also an English version of MacGhille Mhaoil (Macmillan), a clan also known as Clann na Belich.

Bennie
Patronymic from Benjamin or Benedict. Also perhaps in some cases from Gaelic *beinn*, 'mountain', 'mountain dweller'.

Benzie
A name from the Inverurie area.

Bethune *see* **Beaton.**

Bews
An Orkney name, perhaps related to the Scandinavian word *bu*, 'palace'.

Biggar
Craft name, Scots 'builder'. But also location name from Biggar, Lanark-shire, perhaps from Gaelic *beag*, 'small', and *tir*, 'land'.

Biggart
From Old Norse *bygg*, 'barley', and *garth*, 'small farm'. 'Dweller at the barley-croft'.

Bilsland
Probably a location name from Bellsland in Ayrshire.

Binnie
From Gaelic *beinnan*, 'little hill'; 'dweller on the little hill'. A name from Lothian where there was a Binnie estate in Uphall parish.

Birnie
Location name from Birnie, near Elgin, perhaps originally from St Birnie. *See* Kilbirnie.

Birse
Location name from Aberdeenshire, from Scots *birss*, 'bush', 'a bushy place'.

Bissett
From French *bise*, 'brown, tawny', with diminutive -et ending.

Black
Descriptive name, but may go back to Old English *blac*, meaning 'pale', as well as *blaec*, 'black'. When a translation of Gaelic *dubh*, it means black or dark-complexioned. Many Lamonds and MacGregors took this name during the time of proscription.

Blackie
Black, with the diminutive -ie suffix added.

Blain
From Gaelic *blian*, 'the groin'; descriptive name meaning angular, lean.

Blair
From Gaelic, meaning 'dweller on the level fields'. Alistair Blair is a well-known fashion designer.

Blance
A Shetland name, perhaps from French *blanc*, but more likely from the
Scandinavian personal name Bljan.

Boa
From the north of Scotland, perhaps related to Bews.

Boag, Boak
Perhaps from Scots *balk*, 'a boundary ridge', 'dweller by the boundary'.
Also spelt Bogue. David Bogue (1750–1825) was a founder of the British
and Foreign Bible Society.

Boath
Location name from Angus and Ross-shire, from Gaelic *both*, 'house'.

Bogle
Originally a nickname, meaning 'tattered scarecrow, bogle'.

Bogue *see* **Boag.**

Bonar
From Old French *bonair*, 'courteous'.

Borthwick
Location name from Borthwick, near Edinburgh, from Old English *burh*,
'castle', and *wic*, 'village or farm': 'village by the castle'.

Boswell
From Old French *bois*, 'wood', and *ville*, 'town', so originally a location
name. The biographer of Dr Samuel Johnson was James Boswell of
Auchinleck (1740–95).

Bothwell
Location name from Bothwell, Lanarkshire ('Buth's well').

Bowie
From Gaelic *buidhe*, 'yellow'. A descriptive name: 'yellow-faced', 'yellow-
haired'.

Boyd
From Gaelic *buidhe*, 'yellow'. A name particularly associated with Bute
and Ayrshire. The Boyds are a sept of Clan Stewart.

Boyle
From Norman-French Beauville, first found in the twelfth century and
established in Scotland and Ireland.

Braid
Scots, 'broad, wide', from Gaelic *braghaid*, 'neck, gully'. James Braid (1870–1950) was a celebrated golfer who won the Open five times.

Bremner
An incomer's name, 'person from Brabant' (Flanders). A northeast coast name, also found as Brebner. Billy Bremner was one of Scotland's greatest international footballers.

Brewster
Occupation name from Scots 'brewer'. *See also* MacGruer.

Brisbane
From Anglo-French *brise-bane*, 'bone-breaker', a military name.

Broadfoot
A Dumfriesshire name, probably a location name, from a river foot, rather than a descriptive name.

Broatch
Location name from Dumfriesshire, from Broats.

Brock, Brockie
From Old English and Scots *brock*, 'badger'. A nickname.

Brodie
Location name from Brodie, Nairnshire, from Gaelic *brothaich*, 'muddy place'. William (Deacon) Brodie (1741–88) was hanged in Edinburgh on a gallows he had designed.

Brogan
From Gaelic *brog*, 'melancholy', 'sorrowing'.

Brotchie
A Caithness and Orkney name of uncertain origin, perhaps related to Scots *brotch*, a 'clasp' or 'brooch'.

Brown
The second most common surname, after Smith. From Old English *brun*, 'brown', or Brun, a personal name. In Scotland this name may have a Gaelic source, either from Mac a' Bhriuthainn, 'son of the brehon or judge'; or as an English form of Gaelic *donn*, 'brown'. The Scots form Broun is rare.

Brownlie
'Dweller at the brown lea or meadow'.

Bruce
From Bruis or Brux in Normandy. The founder of the family came from
there with William the Conqueror; a descendant came to Scotland and
was granted a lordship by David I. King Robert I was a descendant
through the female line. The royal house of Bruce ended with David II in
1371. James Bruce of Kinnaird (1730–94) was a notable explorer, known
as 'the Abyssinian'.

Bryce, Bryson
From a personal name, the Gaulish St Bricius (5th century), established
in Lennox.

Buchan
Location name from the northeastern district of Buchan (possibly Pictish
in origin). Elspeth Buchan (1738–91) was a notable religious fanatic, 'the
woman of revelations'. The novelist John Buchan (1875–1940) wrote *The
Thirty-Nine Steps* and many other novels.

Buchanan
Location name from the area in Stirlingshire associated with Clan
Buchanan (a Pictish name akin to Buchan, or else from Gaelic *both
chanain*, 'house of the priest'), changed from MacAusalain in the thirteenth century by the chief Gilbrid of that name. George Buchanan
(*c*.1506–1582) was a famous scholar and tutor to the young James VI.

Buck, Buick
From Old English *buc*, 'a buck'. David Dunbar Buick (1850–1910)
founded the Buick motor company in the USA.

Budge
An Orkney and Caithness name, adopted by fugitive Macdonalds in the
late fifteenth century.

Buist
A Fife name, from Scots *buist*, 'box' or 'coffin'. Perhaps a coffin-maker or
carpenter.

Bure *see* **Burr.**

Burniston
Location name, from Burnie's place. Burnie, from Old English and Scots
burn, 'a brook', and *ey*, 'island'.

Burns
From Old English and Scots *burn*; 'dweller by the brook'; also 'warrior',

from Old English *beorn*. In the case of Robert Burns (1759–96), whose father spelt it Burnes or Burness, it has been suggested that the family came from Taynuilt, Argyll, where there was a charcoal-burning house, and when they moved to the east coast (he had a cousin at Montrose), they were called Campbell of Burnhouse, then simply Burness, then Burns.

Burr
An Aberdeenshire name. Also spelt Bure. Perhaps from the same origin as Barr.

Busby
Location name from Busby, Lanarkshire (Scandinavian *busk*, 'bush', and *by*, 'place': 'place of bushes'). Sir Matt Busby (1909–96), the well-known football manager, was born in Lanarkshire.

Byres
From Scots *byre*, 'cowshed'. An East Lothian name from the Lindsay barony of Byres.

C

Cadenhead
Location name from the head of the Caldon Water, Selkirkshire.

Cadger
From Scots *cadger*, a 'porter' or 'carter'. A trade name.

Caie
An Aberdeenshire name, cognate with Welsh Cei (Sir Kay was one of the Knights of the Round Table).

Caird
From Gaelic *ceard*, 'a travelling tinker'.

Cairn, Cairns
From Gaelic *carn*, 'cairn'. 'Dweller by the cairn'. Also Cairnie, Cairney.

Cairncross
Location name from Glenesk in Angus; 'dweller by the cairn with the cross'.

Cairney, Cairnie, Cairns *see* **Cairn.**

Caithness
Location name, from the county. The name has been explained as 'headland of the cats'.

Calder
Location name from the several Calders in Scotland from Gaelic, 'stream in the hazel wood'. Alexander Calder (1898–1976), the US kinetic artist, was of Scots descent.

Caldow
Location name from near Dalbeattie, Dumfriesshire.

Caldwell
From Scots, 'cold spring'. 'Dweller by the cold spring'. Also a location name from Renfrewshire.

Calhoun *see* **Colquhoun.**

Callan
A shortened form of MacAllan.

Callander
Location name from the Perthshire town, from Gaelic roots probably meaning 'the chief's hazel wood' but found almost only in the southwest.

Cameron
Name of the Lochaber clan, from Gaelic *cam*, 'hooked', and *sron*, 'nose'. Camerons are often nicknamed Hooky. But there are also Cameron place names in Fife and Edinburgh, making it a location name in the Lowlands. Richard Cameron (1648–80) was a leading Covenanter whose followers, the Cameronians, gave their name to a Scottish regiment.

Cammack *see* **Gammack.**

Campbell
Name of the great Argyll clan. From Gaelic *cam*, 'crooked', and *beul*, 'mouth'. It has also been derived from French *champ*, 'field', and *bel*, 'beautiful'. Thomas Campbell (1777–1844), born in Glasgow, wrote patriotic verse, such as 'Hohenlinden'. General Sir Colin Campbell (1792–1863) gave distinguished service in the Crimean War and the Indian Mutiny.

Cant
From a Scots, originally Gaelic, word meaning 'strong, lusty'. The cel-

ebrated German philosopher Immanuel Kant (1724–1804) was grandson
of a Scottish immigrant.

Cardno
An Aberdeenshire name, from Cardno, near Fraserburgh, a combination
of Pictish *carden*, 'thicket', with the Gaelic -*ach* ending: originally
Cardenach.

Carlyle
Found from the thirteenth century in the Border area of Dumfries,
indicating one who comes from Carlisle. Thomas Carlyle (1795–1881)
was one of Scotland's great men of letters and Robert Carlyle is a popular
Scottish actor.

Carmichael
'Friend or follower of St Michael'. Also, and chiefly, a location name from
the parish in Lanarkshire.

Carnegie
From Gaelic, 'the fort in the gap'. Andrew Carnegie (1835–1919), the
American ironworks millionaire, emigrated as a young boy from Dun-
fermline.

Carr
Can be from Old English *carr*, a 'moss' or 'marsh'; or Gaelic *cathair*, 'a
fort'; or Gaelic *carr*, 'a rock'. *See also* Ker.

Carrick
From Gaelic *caraig*, 'rock' or 'crag'. 'Dweller by the crag'. (*See* Craig).

Carruthers
From Gaelic *carr*, 'fort', and a proper name, perhaps a form of British
Rhydderch. A name from the southwest.

Carstairs
Location name from Lanarkshire ('Terras's castle').

Carswell
From Scots *carse*, 'moor', and 'well': 'dweller by the moor-spring'. But the
cars- may also be from Old English *caerse*, 'cress': 'cress-spring'.

Caskie
From Gaelic *gasc*, 'hollow'; 'dweller in the hollow place'. Donald Caskie
(1902–83), Scots minister in Paris, was a Resistance hero in the Second
World War.

Cattanach
From Gaelic Cattanaich, 'belonging to Clan Chattan'. The name originates with St Catan, 'Little Cat' in Gaelic.

Catto
A Buchan name, a form of Cattoch.

Chalmers
From Scots *chalmer*, 'a room'. Originally 'son of the room attendant'.
Thomas Chalmers (1780–1847) was the minister who led the Disruption
of the Church of Scotland in 1843.

Cheyne
From French *chene*, 'oak'. A name from the northeast.

Chisholm
Name of an Inverness-shire clan, from Old English *cisel*, 'gravel', and
holm, 'island': 'dwellers on the gravelly island'.

Christal
Scots form of Christopher (Greek 'Christ-bearer', from St Christopher).
Also spelt Chrystal.

Christie
Shortened form of Christian and Christopher. Also Christison, son of
Christie. Especially strong in the northeast.

Cleghorn
Location name from Lanarkshire ('clay house').

Clerk
'Clergyman, scholar'. Also written Clark, Clarke. In Gaelic it became
MacCleary and was often translated back into English as Clarke, forming
septs of various clans including Cameron and MacIntosh.

Cluny, Clunie
'Dweller in the meadow', from Gaelic *cluanag*, 'meadow'.

Clyne
Location name from Sutherland, from Gaelic *claon*, 'slope'; and still
found almost only in the far north.

Cochrane, Cochran
Location name from Renfrewshire. It may mean 'the red parcel of land',
from Celtic origins. Admiral Thomas Cochrane (1775–1860) gave service
to four navies.

Cockburn
'Dweller at the wildfowl brook', although it may also be from the Old
English personal name Colbrand. Alison Cockburn (1713–94), a poet
from Selkirkshire, wrote a version of 'The Flowers of the Forest', and the
Scottish judge Lord Cockburn (1779–1854) was also a writer of note.

Collie
From Gaelic *coille*, 'wood'; 'dweller in the woods'.

Collins
Son of Colin. Colin may be from the Gaelic personal name Cailein or a
shortened form of Nicholas.

Colquhoun
Clan name from the west side of Loch Lomond, meaning 'the narrow
wood' and first found in the mid-thirteenth century. Many Lowland
Colquhouns took the name Cowan. Also spelt Calhoun.

Comrie
Location name from the Perthshire village, from Gaelic *comar*, 'conflu-
ence of rivers'. *See also* MacGregor.

Comyn *see* **Cumming.**

Conn
An Aberdeenshire name, claimed as a branch of Clan Donald (also known
as Siol Cuin).

Conner
A form of Connor. From Gaelic Connchobhar: *conn* meaning wisdom and
cobhair, 'help'. Benjamin Conner was one of Scotland's first locomotive
designers.

Cook
A trade name since the twelfth century; also an English form of Gaelic
MacCuagh.

Corbett
From Old French *corbet*, 'raven'. A name associated with the Tarbat
peninsula.

Cordiner
Cordwainer or shoemaker. Souter is much more frequent; this name is
chiefly from the northeast.

Cormack
'Son of the chariot', i.e. warrior, from Gaelic *corb*, 'chariot', and *mac*, 'son'.

Corrie
'Dweller in or by the hollow', from Gaelic *coire*, 'a hollow place'. A location name from Dumfriesshire.

Coull
Location name from Coull in Aberdeenshire, from Gaelic *cul*, 'hill'; and probably other places.

Coulter
From Gaelic *cul tir*, 'back land'; 'dweller on the back land'.

Couper, Coupar
Forms of cooper or barrel-maker; a craft name. It can also be a location name from Cupar (Fife) and Coupar (Angus).

Coupland
Scots form of Copeland, from Old English *copp*, a peak or hilltop: 'dweller on the high ground'. A name from the Southern Uplands.

Coutts
Location name from Cults in Aberdeenshire, perhaps from a Celtic word cognate with Welsh *coed*, 'wood': 'dweller in the wood'. The Coutts banking family came from Montrose.

Cowan
'Dweller in or by the hollow', from Gaelic *cobhan*, 'a hollow place'. It may also be a form of Gowan and Colquhoun.

Cowden
From Old English/Scots *cu*, 'cow', and *den*, 'valley'. 'Dweller in the cowvalley'.

Cowie
From Old English/Scots *cu*, 'cow', and *ey*, 'island'. 'Dweller on the cow island or river pasture'.

Crab *see* **Craib.**

Cragg *see* **Craig.**

Craib, Crab
Of Flemish origin, from the fourteenth century, mostly found in the northeast.

Craig, Cragg
'Dweller by the cliff or crag'. *See* Carrick.

Craigie
A form of Craig, with the diminutive -ie ending.

Craik
A form of Craig.

Cramond
Location name from Cramond, by Edinburgh ('fort on the Almond').

Cranston
From the Old English name Cran, a nickname from the bird name crane and *-ton*, meaning farm or estate.

Crawford
From Scots *craw*, 'crow', and 'ford'. A location name from Upper Clydesdale. The Crawfords are a sept of the Lindsays.

Crichton
Location name from Crichton, in Edinburgh, from Gaelic *crioch*, 'a boundary', and Scots *-ton*,: 'boundary village'. James 'the Admirable' Crichton (1560–*c*.1582) was a brilliant youth, killed in a duel in Italy

Croan, Crohan
May be from Macrohan, 'son of Rohan', or from Gaelic *cruachan*, 'conical hill'.

Croll
From Scandinavian *kroll*, 'curly-headed'; a nickname from the northeast.

Crombie
From Gaelic *crom*, 'crooked', and *achaidh*, 'field'. 'Dweller on the crooked field'. There were Crombie septs of Clan Donald and Clan Gordon.

Crosbie
Scots form of Crosby: from Scandinavian *kross*, 'cross', and *-by*, 'township'.

Crow
A nickname from the bird name.

Croy
An Orkney name, although perhaps originally from the Inverness-shire village.

Cruden
A location name from Aberdeenshire. Also written Crowden, from 'crow's den', 'valley of crows'.

Cruickshank
Scots form of Crookshank, a nickname meaning 'bow-legged'.

Cullen
From Gaelic *cuilean*, 'a whelp or young dog' (pet name or nickname); or Gaelic *cuilthinn*, 'handsome'; or Gaelic *coillin*, 'little wood'. Also a location name from the town in Banffshire.

Culloch
Nickname from either Gaelic *cullach*, 'boar', or *coileach*, 'cock'.

Culross
Location name from the town in Fife, 'back of the promontory'.

Cumming
May be from Celtic Coman (a personal name); or from Old French personal names, Comin, Cumin. The Comyns became a powerful family in medieval Scotland and claimants to the throne. Bruce slew John Comyn in the Greyfriars Kirk, Dumfries, 1306.

Cunningham
Location name from the Ayrshire district, its origin Celtic but obscure: perhaps associated with Gaelic *cuinneag*, 'milk pail'. Allan Cunningham (1784–1842) was a well-known poet and ballad collector.

Currie
May be from Gaelic *curaidh*, 'hero', or cognate with Corrie. Can be an English form of MacVurich (*see* Murdoch). Also a location name from the village in Midlothian, from Gaelic *curraich*, 'marsh'.

Cursiter
Location name from Cursetter, Orkney, and Aberdeenshire. From Scandinavian *Kur's saeter*, 'farm'.

Cushnie
Location name from Leochel, Aberdeenshire, from Gaelic *cuisneach*, 'frosty': 'the cold place'.

D

Dalgarno
Location name from Dalgarnock, Dumfriesshire. But the surname is
found almost only in Aberdeenshire.

Dalgety
Location name from Fife, its Gaelic elements meaning 'the windy field'.

Dalgleish
From Gaelic *dail*, 'field', and *glaise*, 'stream'. 'Dweller at the brook-field'.
Also spelt Dalglish.

Dallas
Location name from Moray, from Gaelic *dail eas*, 'place by the waterfall'.

Dalrymple
Location name from Ayrshire ('place by the crooked pool').

Dalziel, Dalzell, Dalyell
Location name from Lanarkshire. from Gaelic *dail*, 'field'; the origin of
the 'zell' part is obscure. Now more associated with West Lothian.
General Tam Dalyell (*c*.1615–1685) was the leading royalist general in the
Covenanting wars.

Danskin
Immigrant's name, meaning 'one from Danzig' (Poland). An east-coast
name from the seventeenth century.

Dargie
From Gaelic *dearg*, 'red': 'red-faced' or 'red-haired'.

Darroch
'Dweller at the oak-wood', from Gaelic *darach*, 'oak'.

Davidson
'Son or descendant of David'. May be devotional in origin, from the Biblical
David. The Davidsons were part of the great Clan Chattan confederation of
the central Highlands. The Dawsons were a sept of the Davidsons, from
Badenoch.

Davie
Scots form of David: 'son of David'.

Deans
From Old English/Scots *den*, 'valley': 'dweller in the vale'.

Dearness
Location name from Deerness, Orkney, probably 'dark head' rather than 'deer head'.

Deas
'Incomer from the south', from Gaelic *deas*, 'south'.

Dempster
From Old English *dema*, 'judge'; in Scotland a judge in a baronial court.

Denholm
Location name from Dumfriesshire and Renfrewshire; from Old English/ Scots *den*, 'valley', and *holm*, 'island'.

Denny
'Son of Dennis'; or location name from Stirlingshire.

Denoon
A Ross-shire name, cognate with Dunoon (Gaelic *dun obhainn*, 'fort by the water'); taken in the fifteenth century by a Campbell family fleeing from justice in Argyll.

Deuchar, Deuchart
A location name from the lands of Deuchar in Angus.

Dewar
From Gaelic *deoradh*, 'pilgrim, wanderer'. Perhaps given to one who had made a pilgrimage to a holy place like St Duthac's Chapel in Tain. Sir James Dewar (1842–1923) invented the vacuum flask.

Diack, Dyack
An Aberdeenshire name, possibly a form of Dick but also said to be of Danish origin.

Dick, Dickson
A diminutive of Richard. A Border clan that flourished up to the seventeenth century.

Dingwall
Location name, from the town in Ross-shire. Old Norse *thing-vallr*, 'place of meetings'.

Dinwiddie, Dunwoody
Location name from Dumfriesshire. Gaelic *dun*, 'fort', with obscure ending.

Doak *see* Doig.

Dobbie, Dobie
Diminutive forms of Robert. Also Dobson.

Docherty
'One who suffers', from Gaelic *dochart*, 'difficult, hard to endure'.

Doig
Shortened from Cadoc; originally Gaelic Gille Dog, 'St Cadoc's follower'.
Also found as Doak.

Dollar
Location name from the town in Clackmannanshire. From Gaelic *dal*,
'field;' the *-ar* perhaps indicates ploughed land.

Donn
From Gaelic *donn*, 'brown': 'of brown complexion or hair'.

Donnachie
From Gaelic *donn*, 'brown', and *cath*, 'warrior': 'brown warrior'. The
English form is Duncan.

Donald
One of the names of the great Clan Donald, from Gaelic *domhnuill*,
related to Latin *dominus*, 'lord or master'.

Donaldson *see* Donald, MacDonald.

Dougall
From Gaelic, *dubh*, 'dark', and *gall*, 'stranger or southerner'.

Douglas
From Gaelic *dubh*, 'dark', and *glais*, 'water'; 'dweller at the black water'.
The name of the great Border family since the twelfth century. Sir James
Douglas (*c.*1286–1330) was one of Bruce's lieutenants; Gavin Douglas
(*c.*1474–1522), bishop of Dunkeld, was an author and poet who trans-
lated the *Aeneid*.

Dow
From Gaelic *dubh*, 'dark': 'dark-faced' or 'dark-haired'.

Downie
From Gaelic *dun*, 'hill'. 'Dweller on the hill'.

Drever
Scots form of 'driver' or 'drover': 'a cattle driver'.

Drummond
From Gaelic *druiman*, 'ridge'; 'dweller on the ridge'. George Drummond (1687–1766) is known as the founder of the New Town in Edinburgh.

Dryburgh
Location name from the Border town; perhaps from Old English *dry*, 'wizard', and *burh*, 'fort'.

Duff, Duffy
From Gaelic *dubh*, 'dark or black'; 'of dark complexion'.

Duguid
Scots version of an Anglo-Saxon name, Dogod, meaning to fight for the good; a devotional name.

Dunbar
From Gaelic *dun*, 'a fort', and *barr*, 'a hilltop': 'dweller in the hill fort'. Also a location name from the town in East Lothian. William Dunbar (*c.*1460–*c.*1520), born in East Lothian, is one of Scotland's greatest poets.

Duncan
From old Gaelic *donn*, 'brown', and *cath*, 'warrior': 'brown warrior'. Another derivation gives the meaning 'fortress-head', influenced by its early use as a name for kings. Duncan (*c.*1000–1040) was the first king of all Scotland, slain and defeated by Macbeth.

Dundas
From Gaelic *dun*, 'hill', and *deas*, 'south': 'dweller on the south hill'. Henry Dundas (1742–1811) was virtual ruler of Scotland in the reign of George III.

Dunlop
Location name from Dunlop in Ayrshire, from Gaelic *dun*, 'hill', and *luib*, 'a bend'. John Boyd Dunlop (1840–1921), born in Dreghorn, Ayrshire, invented the pneumatic tyre.

Dunn
From Gaelic *donn*, 'brown'; the name of a Border clan. Also spelt Dunne.

Dunnett
Location name from the district in Caithness. A hybrid word, Gaelic *dun*, 'fort', with Scandinavian *hofud*, 'head'.

Dunning
Location name from the village in Perthshire. It may also be a descriptive name, from Gaelic *donn*, 'brown'.

Dunwoody *see* **Dinwiddie.**

Durie
From Gaelic *durach*, 'watery', meaning watery or marshy land: 'dweller by the marsh'. Also a location name from Durie in Fife. Durie was the name given to the archvillain in Stevenson's *The Master of Ballantrae.*

Durno
Location name from the Aberdeenshire village, from Gaelic *doirneach*, 'stony'.

Durrand
From French *durant*, 'lasting, enduring'.

Durward
From Old English/Scots *dur*, 'door', and *ward*, 'guardian': 'doorkeeper'.

Duthie
From Gaelic *dubh*, 'dark'. Probably a shortened form of MacGille Dubhthaigh, 'follower of St Duthac'.

Dyack *see* **Diack.**

Dyce
Location name from Aberdeenshire, probably from Gaelic *deas*, 'south'.

E

Eachan
From Gaelic Eachann, Hector. A personal name from the Trojan hero (Greek, 'holding fast'); pehaps also as a nickname from Gaelic *eachan*, 'horse'.

Easson, Esson
From Old English *esna*, 'a servant', although Esna was also a personal name. Also from an abbreviation of Adam to Ay.

Eadie, Eddie
From Old English *Ead-*, used in such names as Eadgar (Edgar); shortened
to Edd, with diminutive -ie ending. Also from a pet form of Adam, when
spelt also Addie, Addy.

Edgar
A name from the southwest, from Old English Eadgar, 'happy spear'.

Edleston
Location name from the village near Peebles, from Old English 'Eadwulf's
town'.

Eglinton
Location name from Ayrshire, from Old English, meaning 'seat of the
Aeglings, or Aegel family'.

Elder
From elder tree: 'dweller by the elder tree'; may also stem from elder
meaning older, to designate an elder person of the same name.

Elliott
Originally a French form of Elias; name of a prominent Border family.
Jean Elliott (1727–1805) wrote 'The Flowers of the Forest' and many
other still popular songs.

Elphinstone
Location name from Stirlingshire; 'Elphin's castle'. Elphin may be Celtic
or Old English Aelfwine.

Elrick
A location name from the northeast where there are several Elricks or
Elrigs, from Old Germanic words meaning 'place of ambush'.

Emery *see* **Imrie.**

Erskine
Location name from Renfrewshire; a Celtic name of uncertain origin but
perhaps connected with Gaelic *aird*, 'height'. Henry Erskine (1746–1817)
was well known as a lawyer, orator and wit; his brother Thomas (1750–
1823) was a reforming politician.

Esdaile
Location name, a form of Eskdale. There are several River Esks in Scotland; from Gaelic *uisge*, 'water'.

Esslemont
A location name from Aberdeenshire from the seventeenth century, from Gaelic *eoisle monadh*, 'hill of spells'.

Esson *see* **Easson.**

Eunson
'Son of Ewan'. A well-known name in Orkney. Magnus Eunson was a famous Kirkwall smuggler.

Ewan
'Son of Ewan or Eoghan'. *See also* MacEwan.

Ewing
A form of Ewan. There is also an English form, from the Old English name Eawa.

F

Fairbairn
'The fair-haired child'; a descriptive name.

Falconer
An occupation name: 'the falcon keeper'. Also spelt Faulkner.

Farquhar, Farquharson
From Gaelic *fear*, 'man', and *car*, 'dear or beloved': 'the well-loved one'.

Fearn
Location name from the parish in Ross-shire, from Gaelic *fearn*, 'alder tree': 'dweller by the alders'.

Ferguson
'Son of Fergus'; from Gaelic, meaning 'man of strength', claiming descent from Fergus MacErc, who led the Scots to Dalriada. Also spelt Fergusson. Robert Fergusson (1750–74) was a predecessor of Burns as a poet who wrote in Scots.

Fernie
From Gaelic *fearnach*, 'alders': 'dweller by the alder wood'.

Fiddes
Location name from Foveran, Kincardineshire, from the early thirteenth century, perhaps from Fidach, one of the seven sons of Cruithne, king of the Picts.

Fife, Fyfe, Fyffe
Location name from Fife. Origin of the name is ascribed to Fiobh, son of Cruithne, father of the Picts.

Findlater
From Gaelic *fionn*, 'white, bright', and *leitir*, 'a hillside': 'dweller on the bright hill'. A location name from Banffshire.

Finlay, Findlay
From Gaelic, either as 'fair' (from *fionn*) or Finn's (from Fionn) with *laoch*, 'soldier'. *See* MacKinlay.

Finn, Finnie
From Gaelic *fionn*, 'white' or 'bright', or the proper name Fionn, Finn.

Firth
An Orkney location name, from the parish on Firth Bay, Mainland, from Scandinavian *fjord*, 'a sea inlet'.

Fleck
From Old English and Scots *flek*, 'a mark' or 'spot'; a descriptive name.

Fleming
Incomer from Flanders, often a weaver's name, found especially in weaving communities. Sir Alexander Fleming (1881–1955), born in Loudoun, Ayrshire, discovered penicillin.

Fletcher
'Featherer' or 'fledger of arrows'. Andrew Fletcher of Saltoun (1655–1716) was a patriot Scots politician who strongly opposed the Union of 1707.

Flett
From Scandinavian *fliot*, 'swift, speedy'. A name found in the Northern Isles and Caithness.

Flockhart
A form of the old name Flucker, once common in Fife; perhaps from Frisian Folker, 'of the nation or people'.

Forbes
Location name from Forbes in Aberdeenshire; Old Gaelic *forba*, 'field'.
Duncan Forbes of Culloden (1685–1747) did much to secure the eastern
Highlands for the Hanoverian government in 1745.

Fordoun, Fordun
Location name from Kincardineshire. John Fordoun (died *c.*1384), the
chronicler, is one of the main sources of Scottish history before the
fifteenth century.

Fordyce
From Gaelic *fothar*, 'woodland', and *deas*, 'south'; 'dweller in the south
woodland'. A location name from Banffshire.

Forgan
First part from Gaelic *fothar*, 'woodland'; second part uncertain; also a
location name from Fife.

Forrest
'Dweller in the big wood'.

Forrester
'Forest warden, gamekeeper'.

Forsyth
First part from Gaelic *fothar*, 'woodland'; second part uncertain. It has
also been derived from *fearsidhe*, 'man of peace'. Gordon Forsyth (1879–
1953) was one of the great ceramic designers of the twentieth century.

Forth
Location name from the river and firth, from Old Germanic *foir*, 'boundary, frontier'.

Foubister
Location name from Orkney. Scandinavian, 'Fuba's *saeter*' or 'farm'.

Foulis
Location name from Perthshire and Ross-shire, from Gaelic *folais*, 'burn,
stream'.

Fowlie
Location name from Foulzie in Aberdeenshire.

Fraser
Name of the clan of the Lovat district. Sometimes traced back to Old French

fraise, 'strawberry', also to *frisel*, 'Frisian', from the Dutch North Sea province, and Old French *frise*, 'curled'. Frisell and Frizzell remain as alternative forms, found especially in the Borders. The Fraser river is named after Simon Fraser (1776–1833), an American of Scots descent. Peter Fraser (1884–1950), born in Fearn, was prime minister of New Zealand.

Fullarton, Fullerton
Location name from Ayrshire: 'the fowler's place'.

Fulton
Location name from Fulton, Roxburghshire: most likely 'the fowl yard', but possibly 'Fula's place'.

Fyfe, Fyffe *see* **Fife.**

G

Gair
'Short, small', from Gaelic *gearr*. A descriptive name.

Gairdner
Scots form of Gardner: 'worker in the garden or yard'.

Galbraith
'A southerner or lowlander'; Gaelic *gall*, 'stranger', and *breatannach*, 'Briton'. A name from Stirlingshire and later from the Isle of Gigha where they became a sept of Clan Donald.

Gall
'A foreigner or stranger', from Gaelic *gall*.

Gallay, Galley, Gallie
'A foreigner or stranger' (Gaelic *gall*). Can also come from 'galley-man', 'one who rows in a galley'.

Galloway
One belongng to Galloway, land of the 'stranger Gaels'.

Galpin, Galpern
'Scullion, kitchen-boy' (*cf* French *galopin*, 'errand boy').

Galt
'The hog', from Old Norse *galti*, 'a hog or pig'. A nickname. Can also be from Gaelic *gall*, 'stranger'. John Galt (1779–1839), born in Irvine, was a popular novelist and poet.

Galvin
'Sparrow', from Gaelic *gealbhan*, 'sparrow'.

Gammack
From Gaelic *gamag*, 'a stride'; nickname for a strong walker. Also spelt Cammack.

Gammell *see* Gemmell.

Gammie
Perhaps a form of Gammack; an Aberdeenshire name.

Garden
Perhaps from Scots *car*, 'bog', and *den*, 'valley', with c hardened to g. A name chiefly found in the northeast. Mary Garden (1874–1967) was a famous opera singer.

Gardyne
Location name from Kirkden in Angus, derived as for Garden.

Garioch, Garrioch
Location name from the district, from Gaelic *garbh*, 'rough': 'the rough country'. Found in the Northern Isles as Garriock.

Garrow
'Rough, rude'; 'dweller in the rough country'; from Gaelic *garbh*, 'rough'.

Garry, Garvie *see* Garrow.

Gault, Gauld *see* Galt.

Gavin
Can be either a form of the Welsh name Gwalchmai ('hawk-field') or of Gaelic *gamhainn* ('a calf' or 'stirk'); in the latter case a nickname, meaning calf-head or yokel.

Gay
'Goose', from Gaelic *geadh*.

Geddes
Location name from Nairnshire. Claimed also as a Scottish form of Gideon, the Old Testament Jewish leader. Jenny Geddes (*c.*1600–*c.*1660)

was the instigator of a Protestant riot in church in 1637. Sir Patrick Geddes (1854–1932) was a pioneer of modern town planning.

Geikie, Geekie
Location name from Gagie in Fife. Sir Archibald Geikie (1835–1924) was a distinguished geologist.

Gemmell
From Middle English and Scots *gamel*, 'old'. 'The old one'. A name found widely in the south. Also spelt Gammell.

Georgeson
'Son of George'. George was originally a name for a land worker, from Greek *georgos*, 'farmer'.

Gibb
Shortened form of Gilbert. Gibbon was also a pet form of Gilbert.

Gilbert, Gilbertson
Through Norman French from Scandinavian *gisel*, 'pledge' or 'hostage', and *bjart*, 'bright, shining'.

Gilchrist
'Servant or follower of Christ', from Gaelic *gille*, 'servant'.

Gill, Giles
'Servant' or 'follower', from Gaelic *gille*, 'servant'.

Gillanders
'Follower of St Andrew' (a sept of Clan Ross).

Gillespie
'Servant or follower of a bishop', from Gaelic *gille easbuig*. A sept of Clan Macpherson. Used as a Gaelic form of Archibald on the supposition that *bald* ('bold') meant a cleric's shaven pate. *See also* Archibald.

Gillies
'Follower of Jesus', from Gaelic *gille Iosa*.

Gilmour
'Follower of Mary', from Gaelic *gille Mhuire*. A sept of Clan Morrison from the Isle of Lewis. Also spelt Gilmore.

Gilroy, Gilderoy
'Servant of the red-haired one'. Gilderoy was a well-known Perthshire bandit.

Girvan
Location name from Ayrshire; the name of the town means 'short river', Gaelic *gearr abhainn*.

Glaister
Craft name, 'a glazier, glass-maker'.

Glasgow
Location name; from Glasgow, probably from Old Gaelic *glas cau*, 'green hollows'.

Glass
'Pale-faced', from Gaelic *glas*. Can also be 'dweller by the stream' (Gaelic *glas*).

Glasson
A form of Glass. The ending -an or -on is a diminutive in Gaelic.

Glegg
'Clever, sharp', from Old Norse, *glegg*.

Glen, Glenn, Glennie
'Valley-dweller', from Gaelic *gleann*, 'valley'. Evelyn Glennie is a celebrated percussionist.

Glendenning, Glendinning
Location name from Dumfriesshire: 'valley of the white hill'.

Gloag
From Old Germanic *glocke*, *glogge*, 'bell'; the sixteenth-century forms were Glook and Gloog.

Glover
Trade name, 'glove-maker'. Scott's Fair Maid of Perth was Catherine Glover.

Goldie, Goudy, Goudie
Gold, from Old English and Scots *gold*, possibly a descriptive name relating to hair colour.

Goodlad
Originally mainland, now a Shetland name; its meaning is good fellow: a nickname or servant's name.

Gordon
Location name from Gordon, Berwickshire, from Old Gaelic *gor dun*, 'hill fort', although far more identified with the Gordon district in Aberdeen-

shire from 1357 onwards, when the laird of Gordon was granted Strathbogie, now the centre of the territory of the clan Gordon. Many local clans were absorbed and took the Gordon name.

Goudie, Goudy *see* **Goldie.**

Gourlay
From Old English *gore*, a triangular piece of land, and *ley*, 'field': 'dweller by the gore field'; perhaps a now-lost location name.

Gow
From Gaelic *gobha*, 'smith'. Niel Gow (1727–1807), born near Dunkeld, was a celebrated violinist and songwriter. *See also* MacGowan.

Gowan
From Gaelic *gobha, gobhainn*, 'smith'.

Gracie
From French *gras*, 'fat', with diminutive -ie ending; a nickname. But *see also* Grassick.

Graham
From Old English and Scots *graeg*, 'grey', and *ham*, 'enclosure', but perhaps a location name from Grantham in England, whence the de Grahams came to Scotland in the twelfth century. James Graham (1612–50), Marquis of Montrose, was one of Scotland's greatest men – a soldier, courtier and poet.

Grant
From Norman French *grand*, 'large'. The clan Grant's territory is in the uplands of Banffshire. Duncan Grant (1885–1978), the painter, was born near there in Rothiemurchus. *See also* MacGregor.

Grassick
From Gaelic *greusaich*, 'shoemaker', most common in Aberdeenshire and the Mearns. Grassie is a form of this name.

Gray
The usual Scots spelling of the descriptive name Grey.

Greer *see* **Grier.**

Greig, Gregor
Scots forms of Gregg, from old Gaelic *giric*, 'king's crest'; later confused with Latin *gregorius*, 'watchman'.

Grier, Grierson, Greer
A shortened form of Gregor, Gregorson, in use from the time when MacGregor as a name was proscribed.

Grieve
'A farm bailiff'. Christopher Murray Grieve was the original name of Hugh MacDiarmid (1892–1978), born in Langholm, one of the major poets of the twentieth century.

Groat
From Dutch *groot*, 'great'; a name from Orkney and Shetland.

Grosset
A form of Grosart, from Old German *grossartig*, 'generous'.

Groundwater
An Orkney location name, from Orphir, Mainland.

Gunn
Name of a Caithness clan, from the Scandinavian name Gunnar, 'warrior'. Neil Gunn (1891–1973), born in Dunbeath, was one of Scotland's great novelists.

Guthrie
Location name from Angus; from Gaelic *gaothair*, 'wind': 'the windy place'.

H

Haddo
Location name from Aberdeenshire, meaning 'half a davoch' (unit of land measurement).

Haig
From Old English *haga*, 'hedge': 'dweller within the hedge or enclosure'.

Halcrow, Halcro
An Orkney name from South Ronaldsay, from a Scandinavian personal name, first recorded in 1492.

Haldane
From Scandinavian *half-dan*, 'half-Dane': someone with one Danish

parent but also found as a location name in the twelfth century, from the manor of Hauden. J. B. S. Haldane (1892–1964), biologist, wrote books on science and ethics.

Halliday
From holy day; 'one born on a holy day'; mostly found in the southwest.

Hamilton
Location name from Lanarkshire, from the Norman-French name de Hameldon. Patrick Hamilton (1503–28) was a martyr for the Protestant cause.

Hannay, Hanna
Perhaps from Gaelic O *hAnnaidh*, one of the few Scots patronymics beginning with O'; a Galloway name. The Hanna form is more often found in Ireland.

Hardie
Scots form of English Hardy, 'bold, daring'. James Keir Hardie (1856–1915) was the first Labour MP.

Harcus
A form of Harcarse ('hare moor'), a location in Berwickshire but now found almost only in Orkney. Also spelt Harkess.

Harkness
From Scandinavian *horg*, 'a place of worship', and *nes*, 'a headland': 'dweller at the temple-headland', but its history suggests it is a name from inland Dumfriesshire.

Harper
A craft name, 'harp-player'. Found mostly in the north and Northern Isles. *See also* MacWhirter.

Harvie, Harvey
From Old English *here*, 'army', and *wig*, 'war': a military name brought by the Normans. Sir George Harvey (1806–76) was a successful painter of Scottish scenes and activities.

Hastie
Old English and Scots 'impetuous, bold'. A nickname.

Hatherwick *see* **Hedderwick.**

Hawthorn
'Dweller by the hawthorn tree'.

Hay
From Old English *haeg, haga*, 'a hedge' or 'enclosure': 'dweller by the hedge'. The lands of the clan Hay are around Errol in Perthshire. John MacDougall Hay (1881–1919) from Tarbert was a minister and the author of a powerful novel, *Gillespie*. His son, George Campbell Hay (1915–84), became a prominent Gaelic poet.

Hedderwick
From Scots and Old English *hedder*, 'heather', and *wick*, 'farm' or 'place': 'dweller on the heath'. Also spelt Hatherwick.

Henderson
'Son of Hendry' (a form of Henry showing Scandinavian or Dutch influence). Lowland Hendersons are traced back to Henryson; in Caithness they are a branch of Clan Gunn, from a fifteenth-century split.

Hendry
Scots form of Henry.

Henryson
'Son of Henry'. Robert Henryson (*c.*1425–1508) of Dunfermline was a poet, author of *The Testament of Cresseid*.

Hepburn
From Old English *hepe*, 'the dog-rose', and *burn*: 'dweller by the dog-roses'. Originally from Hebburn in Northumberland, they became a powerful Lothian family.

Herd, Hird
Scots 'herdsman, shepherd'.

Heriot
Location name from Heriot in Midlothian, meaning either 'the hares' place' (from Norman French) or the Old English legal word *h'eriot*, meaning 'a military outfit'. George Heriot (1523–1624), known as 'Jingling Geordie', was the Edinburgh goldsmith and moneylender who helped finance King James VI and I. Also spelt Herriot.

Hislop, Hyslop
From hazel (Scandinavian *hasl*) and *hope*, 'a hollow': 'dweller in the hazel grove'. The form Heslop is found mostly in the northeast.

Hogg
A nickname or occupational name. 'Hog' or 'hogg' could refer to a

castrated boar, a young sheep or a colt. James Hogg (1770–1835), 'the Ettrick Shepherd', was a gifted poet and novelist.

Holm, Holme
From Scandinavian *holm*, 'island': 'island dweller'. A name from the Black Isle and other northern districts.

Home, Hume
May be from the same source as Holm or from the English *holm*, 'holly tree', also holm oak. But Home is a Border name. Grizel Hume (1665–1746) was a poet and songwriter, and a heroine of the Covenanters. David Hume (1711–76) is Scotland's most eminent philosopher.

Honeyman
Occupation name, 'a beekeeper'. Associated mostly with Fife.

Hope
In the south, from Old English *hop*, 'a valley'; in the north, from Scandinavian *hop*, 'a small bay or inlet of the sea'.

Horne
From Scandinavian Horn, both a personal name and '(drinking) horn'. Found in the northeast.

Hosie
From Old English and Scots *hose*, *hoose*, 'a house', with diminutive -ie ending. 'Dweller in the (large) house'.

Hossack
A name from the northern counties, of uncertain origin; possibly the Gaelic diminutive *-ag* attached to Scots *hoose*: 'dweller in the small house'.

Houston
Location name from Renfrewshire ('Hugh's town'). Samuel Houston (1793–1863), who gave his name to the Texas city, was of Scottish descent.

Howat, Howatson
From Scandinavian *how*, 'hill': 'dweller on the hill'.

Hoy
Location name from the Orkney island, from Scandinavian *ha*, 'high', and *ey*, 'island': 'the high island'.

Hughes, Hughson
'Son of Hugh'. Hughson is found mostly in Shetland and the Western Isles.

Hume *see* **Home.**

Hunter
Occupational name, 'hunter', but linked mainly with Ayrshire. John Hunter (1728–93) was the founder of modern surgery; his brother William (1718–83), the anatomist, was founder of the Hunterian Museum in Glasgow.

Hutcheson
Scots form of Hutchinson: 'son of Hutchin' (a form of Hugo). Francis Hutcheson (1694–1746), philosopher, was born in Ulster, of Scottish descent.

Hyslop *see* **Hislop.**

I

Imrie, Imray
Shortened forms of the old name Amalric, found from the fourteenth century. Also spelt Emery.

Inch
From Gaelic *inis*, 'island': 'island dweller'.

Inglis
From Scots Englis, Inglis, a name given to an incomer from England. Elsie Inglis (1864–1917) was a pioneer in women's medicine.

Inkster
A Shetland name, a form of Ingsetter, 'dweller on Ing's farm'.

Innes
From Gaelic *inis*, 'island': 'island dweller'.

Irvine, Irving
Location name from the Ayrshire town and the Dumfriesshire district.

Originally a river name, possibly 'brown' or 'white river', depending on the source being Gaelic *odhar*, 'brown', or Celtic *wyn*, 'white'.

Isbister
Location name from Orkney, Scandinavian 'Ine's *bolstadr*', or 'place'.

J

Jack
A name from Avoch in the Black Isle, perhaps connected with the Scandinavian name Jak or French Jacques; also found in the northeast and southwest.

Jameson, Jamieson
'Son of James'. There were Jamiesons on Bute, on the Border, and also associated with Clan Gunn in Caithness. George Jamesone (*c.*1588–1644) was one of the first Scottish portrait painters.

Japp, Jappy
From Dutch Jaap, a form of Jacob. An east-coast name.

Jardine
From Old French *jardin*, 'garden'. 'Dweller by the garden or orchard'.

Johnston, Johnstone
Scots form of Johnson, 'son of John'. John was for centuries the most common male first name. It can also be a location name from the Renfrewshire town and the Johnstone estate in Dumfriesshire, where the Johnstones were a notable reiving clan. *See also* MacIan.

Jolly, Jollie
From Old French *joli*, 'merry, gay'. Also spelt Joly.

Joss
A name from the northeast, perhaps connected with French Josse, the name of a Breton saint. Found from the fourteenth century on.

Junor
A form of Jenner, from Middle English *engynour*, 'one who works with war machines'.

K

Kay
A contracted form of MacKay.

Keiller
Location name from the River Keilor in Angus. Originally as Calder, 'stream in the wood'.

Keir
From Gaelic *ciar*, 'dark'; 'dark-complexioned'. James Keir (1735–1820), chemist, was one of the creators of the Industrial Revolution.

Keith
Location name from the Banffshire town (there is also an East Lothian Keith). May be from Old Gaelic Cait, legendary son of Cruithne, father of the Picts, or Old Gaelic *coit*, 'wood'. James Keith (1696–1785) became a fieldmarshal in the Prussian army.

Keldie, Kelday
An Orkney name, from Keldall in Holm.

Kelman
An Aberdeenshire name, from Gaelic *calma*, 'stout'.The writer James Kelman won the Booker Prize in 1993.

Kelty, Keltie
Location name from the town in Fife: Gaelic *coille*, 'woods'.

Kelvin
Location name from the Glasgow river, from Gaelic *caol*, 'narrow', and *abhainn*, 'river'. Lord Kelvin (1824–1907), the famous scientist, was in fact named Alexander Thomson.

Kemp
From Scandinavian *kempa*, 'warrior', although it may have come through Old English.

Kennaway *see* **Kennoway.**

Kennedy
An Ayrshire name, brought from Ireland and re-exported there. From Gaelic *ceann*, 'head', and *eidigh*, 'ugly': a nickname.

Kenneth
Gaelic C*oinneach*, meaning 'fair one'. *See* MacKenzie.

Kennoway
Location name from Fife; Gaelic *ceann*, 'head', and *aichean*, 'fields': 'head of the fields'. Also spelt Kennaway. James Kennaway (1928–68) was a well-known novelist and scriptwriter.

Kerr, Ker
'Dweller at the fort', from Gaelic *carr*, 'fortress'; although it can also derive from Scandinavian *carr*, 'marsh', or Gaelic *ciar*, 'dusky' (the Kerrs of Arran). Mostly a Border name. Alternative spellings are Carr, Curr, Karr. Deborah Kerr (born 1921), actress, was born in Helensburgh.

Kidd
From Scandinavian *kid*, 'young goat'; a nickname.

Kilbirnie
Location name from the Ayrshire town; from Gaelic *cill*, 'chapel', and St Birnie.

Kilbride
Location name from the Argyll parish; from Gaelic *cill*, 'chapel', and St Bride (Bridget). May also be a form of Gilbride, 'follower of Bridget'.

Kilgour
From Gaelic *coille*, 'a wood', and *gobhar*, 'goat': 'dweller in the goats' wood'.

Kilpatrick
From Gaelic *cill*, 'chapel', and St Patrick: 'dweller by Patrick's chapel'. A location name from Dumbartonshire.

Kindness
An Aberdeenshire name, perhaps a shortened, anglicised form of MacInnes.

King
Perhaps originally 'king's man'. Found from the thirteenth century, often taken by clansmen who left the Highlands.

Kinloch
From Gaelic *ceann*, 'head', and 'loch': 'dweller at the head of the loch'.

Kinnaird
From Gaelic *ceann*, 'head', and *aird*, 'hill': 'dweller on the hill head'.

Kinneil
Location name from West Lothian. From Gaelic *ceann*, 'head', and *fhaill*, 'wall': 'end of the wall' (Antonine's Wall).

Kinneir, Kinnear
From Gaelic *ceann*, 'head', and *iar*, 'west': 'dweller on the western hill'.

Kippen
Location name from Stirlingshire; from Gaelic *ceap*, 'tree stump'.

Kirkcaldy
Location name from the town in Fife, from Gaelic *cathan*, 'fort', and a proper name, Calatin. Sir William Kirkcaldy of Grange (*c*.1520–1573) was a prime mover in the political struggles of the sixteenth century.

Kirkness
From Scandinavian *kirkia*, 'church', and *nes*, 'headland': 'dweller by the church on the headland'. Christian version of Harkness.

Kirkpatrick
Scots form of Kilpatrick. A location name from Dumfriesshire.

Kitto
From Gaelic *ciotach*, 'left-handed'. A descriptive name.

Knox
From Gaelic *cnoc*, 'a hill', with the English addition of -s. The name seems to have originated in Renfrewshire, where lived the ancestors of John Knox (*c*.1513–72), the Protestant reformer.

Kyle
From Gaelic *caol*, 'strait' or 'narrow': 'dweller by the strait'. There are many Kyles but the foremost as a location name is the north Ayrshire district.

L

Lachlan *see* **MacLachlan.**

Lackie, Leckie
From Gaelic *leacach*, 'flagstones': 'dweller in the stony place'.

Lagan, Laggan
From Gaelic *lag*, 'a hollow': 'dweller in the hollow place'.

Laidlaw
From Scots 'lade', 'a waterway', and 'law', 'hill': 'dweller at the stream by the mound'.

Laing *see* **Lang.**

Laird
From Scots *laird*, 'a landowner'.

Lamberton
Location name from Berwickshire. 'Dweller in Lambert's town'. Lambert was a common name among the Norman French.

Lambie
Scots form of Lamb, a nickname or pet name.

Lamington
Location name from Lanarkshire; 'Lamkin's place'.

Lamond, Lamont
Name of an Argyll clan. Originally Scandinavian, from *log*, 'law', and *mann*, 'man': 'lawgiver'. The Gaelic form is MacErchar. *See also* Whyte.

Lang, Laing
Scots form of Long. A descriptive name. Andrew Lang (1844–1912) was a writer and collector of fairy tales.

Lauder
Location name from the Border valley and town. From Old Gaelic *lothur*,

'a trench'. Sir Harry Lauder (1870–1950) remains the archetypal Scottish comedian

Laurie, Lawrie
A Scots form of Laurence, either from French Laurence or from the martyr St Lawrence – a dedicational name.

Law
From Scots *law*, 'hill': 'dweller on or by the hill'. John Law (1671–1729), financier and speculator, was a pioneer of modern banking methods. Also Lawson.

Lea, Lee
From Gaelic *liath*, 'grey'; 'grey-haired'.

Leach *see* **Leitch.**

Leask
A Shetland name but originally from Leask in Aberdeenshire, now Pitlurg.

Leckie *see* **Lackie.**

Lees, Leeson
A shortened form of Gillies.

Leiper
A form of Leaper, from Old English *leapere*, 'basket-maker'. A craft name found only in Aberdeenshire.

Leishman
From Scots *leish*, 'active, nimble', with -man added. Sir William Leishman (1865–1926) discovered a vaccine against typhoid.

Leitch
Scots form of Old English *leech*, 'physician'. Also spelt Leach.

Leith
Location name from Midlothian; from Gaelic *leath*, 'wide' (river).

Lennie
From Gaelic *leana*, 'marsh-pasture': 'dweller by the water meadows'.

Lennox
Location name from Dumbartonshire; from Gaelic *leamhanach*, 'elm trees'.

Leslie

From Gaelic *lios*, 'enclosure', and *liath*, 'grey': 'dweller in the grey enclosure', from Leslie in Aberdeenshire but mostly a Fife name, from the town of Leslie. Alexander Leslie (*c*.1580–1661), first Earl of Leven, became a Swedish field marshal and led the Covenanting army.

Leven

Location name from the Levens in Fife and Dumbarton. From Gaelic *leamhan*, 'elm tree': 'place of elms'.

Leys

Location name from Leys in Inverness-shire; from Old English/Scots *ley*, 'meadow'.

Liddel, Liddell

Location name from the River Liddel (Roxburghshire). Related to Gaelic *leath*, "broad'. Eric Liddell (1902–45), 'The Flying Scotsman', was an Olympic gold medallist who became a missionary.

Lindsay

Probably of Norman-French origin, from de Limesay in Normandy but possibly from or via Lindsey in Lincolnshire. The name appears in the twelfth century. Their territory was the uplands of Angus.

Linklater

A well-known Orkney name, from several locations called Linklet. Eric Linklater (1899–1974), the novelist, was of Orkney descent.

Lithgow

Location name from Linlithgow; from Gaelic *linne*, 'a lake', and Liathcu, a personal name, meaning 'grey dog'. Or from British *llyn lled cu*, 'dear wide lake'.

Livingstone

Location name from the town in West Lothian (spelt Livingston). From the Old English name Leofing and 'stone', indicating a stone building or castle. David Livingstone (1813–73), missionary and explorer, was born not far away at Blantyre.

Loch

From Gaelic *loch*, 'dweller by the lochside'.

Lochhead

'Dweller at the head of the loch', *see* Kinloch.

Lockerbie
Location name from the Dumfriesshire town; from Scandinavian personal name Loki and -*by*, 'a township'.

Lockhart
From Gaelic *luchairt*, 'castle' or 'palace': 'dweller in or by the castle'. John Gibson Lockhart (1794–1854) was the biographer of Sir Walter Scott.

Logan
From Gaelic *lagan*, 'a hollow': 'dweller in the hollow'. *See also* Lagan. An Ayrshire name, but the Highland Logans may be a separate group, founders of the MacLennans.

Logie
As for Logan; also location name from a number of Logie place names.

Longmuir, Langmuir
Scots form of Longmoor: 'dweller on the long moor'.

Lorimer
A craft name, a maker of the metal parts of harness, bits and spurs. Sir Robert Lorimer (1864–1929), architect, maintained and developed the traditions of Scots architecture.

Lorne
Location name from the Agyllshire district; from the Gaelic name Loarn, 'fox-like'; a legendary chieftain of the Scots.

Lothian
Location name from Lothian; the source of this ancient name is obscure: it may go back to a Celtic personal name.

Loudon
Location name from Ayrshire (spelt Loudoun); from Gaelic *loch* and *dun*, either 'hill' or 'fort'. John Loudon (1783–1843) was an eminent horticulturist and architectural designer.

Love, Lovie
From Old French *love*, 'wolf'. Also spelt Luff. With diminutive -ie it is found in the northeast.

Lown, Lownie
From Scots *loon*, 'a boy'.

Luff *see* Love.

Lumsden
Location name from Berwickshire: 'Lumm's valley'.

Lyall
A shortened form of Lionel. Also written Lyell. Sir Charles Lyell (1797–1875) was one of the fathers of modern geology.

Lyle
Scots form of Lisle, from French *l'ile*, 'an island': 'dweller on the island'.

Lyon
The lion has been a heraldic symbol of Scotland since the thirteenth century, but this associative name is likely to have come from France. The Lyons were centred in Strathmore.

Mac

Mac, Mc, M'
In this dictionary, all these prefixes are treated as Mac-, as the correct form of Gaelic *mac*, 'son of'. This is not to suggest it is the only or even the most appropriate form but simply to avoid duplication. Many of these names are spelt with a Mc or M' prefix by their owners. It is also a matter of personal tradition whether the proper name part begins with a capital letter or not.

MacAdam
'Son of Adam', an Ayrshire name but often taken by MacGregors and others. John Loudon MacAdam (1756–1836), inventor, revolutionised road-building.

MacAfee *see* **MacPhee.**

MacAlister
'Son of Alistair or Alexander'. One of the main branches of Clan Donald, centred on Kintyre and Bute.

MacAllan
'Son of Allan'. There were MacAllans in Aberdeenshire and Sutherland, linked there with the MacKays.

MacAlpin, MacAlpine
'Son of Alpin'. A Perthshire clan, tracing its origin to King Kenneth MacAlpine of the Scots.

MacAndrew
'Son of Andrew'.

MacAngus
'Son of Angus'.

MacAra
'Son of the charioteer'. A sept of Clan MacGregor in western Perthshire.

MacArdle
'Son of Ardghail, the superbrave'.

MacArthur
'Son of Arthur'. An Argyll clan based in Lorne.

MacAskill
'Son of Asketil', from Scandinavian, meaning 'vessel of sacrifice'. From Skye and the Hebrides.

MacCaskie
A Galloway name but cognate with MacAskill, -askie being a form of Asketil.

MacAulay
'Son of Aulay', Gaelic *Amalghaidh*. A Lewis sept of Clan MacLeod, also a Dumbartonshire clan.

MacAusland
'Son of Absalon or Auslan'. A Dumbartonshire clan allied to the Buchanans.

MacBain
'Son of the fair one'. From the northeast.

MacBean
'Son of Beathan', from Gaelic *beatha*, 'life'. St Beathan was a Celtic saint about whom little is known. A Perthshire clan.

MacBeth, MacBeath
Unusual in that it means 'son of life', i.e. man of religion, priest, rather than a personal name. Macbeth (*c.*1005–57), king of Scotland, was mormaer, or earl, of Moray, and it remains a northern name.

MacBey
A form of Macbeth, also spelt MacVay, MacVey. James McBey (1883–1959) was a gifted artist and etcher.

MacBrayne
'Son of the judge' or 'brehon'. This was a hereditary post. Also spelt MacBrain. A Hebridean clan. David MacBrayne set up public transport in the West Highlands and Hebrides.

MacCabe
'Son of Caibe'. An Arran clan that largely migrated to Ireland in the fourteenth century.

MacCaffie, MacHaffie
A Wigtownshire clan, sons of the followers of St Cathbad.

MacCaig
'Son of Tadhg', the poet. A name from the southwest and the Western Isles. Norman MacCaig (1910–1996) was one of the great Scottish poets of the twentieth century.

MacCall
'Son of Cathal' (warrior). A Nithsdale clan.

MacCallion
A form of MacCailin, 'son of Colin'. An Argyll name; the chief of Clan Campbell was MacCailein Mor. Easily confused with MacAllan.

MacCallum
From MacGille Chaluim, 'son of the servant of Colum' (Columba). A clan of Perthshire and Lennox. *See also* Malcolm.

MacCandless, MacCandlish
A Galloway name, from MacCuindleas, 'son of Cuindleas', an ancient Irish name.

MacCarracher *see* **MacKercher.**

MacCartney
A Galloway name, a form of MacArtan, 'son of Art', a personal name from Old Gaelic *art,* 'a bear'.

MacClatchie *see* **MacLatchie.**

MacCleary
From Mac a Cleirich, 'son of the clerk or priest'. Often altered to Clark or Clerk.

MacClelland
From MacGille Fhaolain, 'son of the servant of St Fillan'. A Kirkcudbrightshire name.

MacClintock
From MacGille Fhionndaig, 'son of the servant of St Findan'. A clan of the west side of Loch Lomond and of Lorne in Argyll.

MacClode, MacCloud *see* MacLeod.

MacClung
A Galloway name, from MacCluing, 'son of the ship': a seaman.

MacClure
A Galloway name from MacGille Uidhir, 'son of the servant of Odhar'. Also spelt MacLure, MacAleer. Also a Harris sept of MacLeod, from MacGille Leabhair, 'son of the servant of the book'.

MacClymont
A Galloway name, a form of MacLamond, from MacLaomuinn, 'son of the lawman'. *See also* Lamond.

MacCodrum
From MacCodrum, 'son of Codrum', a personal name from Scandinavian Guttorm, 'divine serpent'. This Uist sept of MacDonald was known as Sliochd nan Ron, 'the people of the seals', from an alleged descent from seal folk.

MacColl
From MacColla, 'son of Coll'. A clan from Appin in Argyll, followers of the Stewarts of Appin.

MacColm
Derived as MacCallum, but this clan is from the southwest.

MacCombie
From MacThomaidh, 'son of Thomas', and often anglicised to Thomson. From the northeast.

MacConachie
From MacDhonnchaidh, 'son of Duncan'. Donnachie is the Gaelic name of the Robertsons of Atholl, although there were also MacConachies on Bute.

MacCorkindale *see* MacCorquodale.

MacCormack
From MacCormaig, 'son of the chariot driver'.

MacCorquodale, MacCorkindale
From the Scandinavian personal name Thorketil ('Thor's kettle'), Gaelic MacCorcadail. An Argyll and west Perthshire clan.

MacCosh
From MacCoise, 'son of the footman', or 'messenger'. An Ayrshire name.

MacCoy *see* **MacKay.**

MacCracken
A Galloway form of MacNaughton, brought from Kintyre.

MacCrae *see* **MacRae.**

MacCrimmon
From the Scandinavian name Hromund, 'famed protector'; Gaelic MacCruimein. From Skye, where the MacCrimmons were hereditary pipers to the chiefs of MacLeod and the leading piping family.

MacCrindle
A form of MacRanald, from the southwest.

MacCubbin
A form of MacGibbon, from the southwest.

MacCulloch
From MacCullaich, 'son of the boar'. A Galloway name, but there were also MacCullochs in Easter Ross

MacCunn
A Galloway form of MacEwen.

MacCurdy *see* **MacKirdie.**

MacCutchen, MacCutcheon
'Son of Hutcheon', from French Huchon, 'little Hugh', originally MacHutchen. The Macdonalds of Sleat are called Clann Uisdean (Gaelic form of Huchon), but the name is largely found in Galloway.

MacDavid
The Gaelic form of Davidson, found mostly in the north.

MacDiarmid
From MacDhiarmaid, 'the son of Dermid'. A clan from Glen Lyon in Perthshire.

MacDonald
From Mac Domhnuill, 'son of Donald'. The most numerous clan name and in all its forms the third most common surname in the country. The great Clan Donald of the Western Isles absorbed many small clans and branched itself off into separate groups, like the MacDonalds of Glencoe, Glengarry and Keppoch. Variants of the same name include MacDonnell and MacConnell. Flora Macdonald (1722–90) was a Jacobite heroine; James Ramsay Macdonald (1866–1937) was Britain's first Labour prime minister.

MacDonnell
See MacDonald. This form was used by the Ulster branch but was also used in Scotland, especially by MacDonald of Glengarry.

MacDougal, MacDougall
From MacDhughaill, 'son of Dougal'. Descended from Somerled, Lord of the Isles; an Argyll clan.

MacDowell
A Galloway form of MacDougal.

MacDuff
From Mac Dhuibh, 'son of Dubh', a personal name related to *dubh*, 'dark'. A clan from Banffshire, although the MacDuffs were earls of Fife. They were regarded as part of the ancient Celtic nobility, and it was as a MacDuff that the Countess of Buchan crowned Robert I in 1306.

MacErchar *see* Lamond; MacKercher.

MacEwan
From Mac Eoghainn, 'son of Ewan'. A clan from Lennox and also Galloway. Often spelt MacEwen. Elspeth MacEwan was the last witch executed in Scotland, in Galloway, 1698.

MacFadyen, MacFadzean
From Mac Phaidean, 'son of little Patrick'. A clan from Mull and Tiree. The z here, as in other old Scottish names, is properly a y and pronounced accordingly.

MacFall *see* MacPhail.

MacFarlane
From Mac Pharlain, 'son of Parlan', a Gaelic form of Bartholomew. The stronghold of the clan was around the north end of Loch Lomond.

MacFarquhar
From Mac Fhearchair, 'son of Farquhar'. Perhaps originally from Kintyre.

MacFee *see* MacPhee.

MacGarry, MacGarrie
From Old Gaelic Mac Fhearadhaigh, 'son of Feredach', a personal name. A Galloway name, also spelt MacHarry, MacHarrie.

MacGarva
From MacGairbheith, 'son of Garvey', a personal name. A Galloway name, also spelt MacGarvie, MacGarvey.

MacGhie, MacGhee
From MacAodh, 'son of Aodh' (*see also* MacKay). A Galloway clan. Also spelt MacKie, MacKee.

MacGibbon
'Son of Gibbon', a pet form of Gilbert. Recorded in Tiree, but it seems to have been chiefly a Perthshire name.

MacGill
From Mac an ghoill, 'son of the stranger'. A Galloway name, although there were also MacGills on Jura. James McGill (1744–1813) emigrated to Canada where he made his fortune and endowed McGill University.

MacGillivray
From MacGille-bhrath, 'son of the servant of judgement'. Originally from Mull.

MacGowan
From Mac Ghobhainn, 'son of the smith'. A widespread name in small numbers; it has often been anglicised to Smith or reduced to Gow.

MacGraw
A form of Irish MacGrath, from macGraith, 'son of Craith', a personal name.

MacGregor
From MacGriogair, 'son of Gregory'. This papal name was a popular baptismal one before the Reformation (sixteenth century). The MacGregors occupied the area between Aberfoyle and Balquhidder; the name was forbidden by Parliament in 1603, and the clansfolk took various other names, including Stewart, Grant, Comrie, Black and Whyte or White. *See also* Gregor.

MacGruer, MacGruther
From Mac Grudaire, 'son of the brewer'; a hereditary trade name, not a patronymic. A name from south Perthshire, although also found as a sept of the Clan Fraser. Anglicised to Brewster.

MacGuffic
A Galloway name, a form of MacGuffog.

MacGuffog
Perhaps a form of Mac Dhabhog, 'son of Davuc', a shortened form of David. Once a prominent Galloway clan, now more commonly found as MacGuffie.

MacGuire
From Mac Uidhir, 'son of the pale-faced one', a descriptive name. From Ayrshire. *See also* MacQuarie.

MacHaffie *see* **MacPhee.**

MacHardie, MacHardy
From Mac Cardaidh, 'son of the sloe', an associative name from the Aberdeenshire uplands.

MacHarg
A form of Irish MacGurk, from macOirc, a personal name.

MacHarrie, MacHarry
From Mac Fearadaigh, 'son of Fearadaigh', a personal name; an Ayrshire name from Carrick. *See* MacGarry.

MacHattie
Now a name from the northeast but originally from Galloway, from mac Cathain, 'son of Cathan'.

MacIan
From Mac Iain, 'son of John'. The clan territory was Ardnamurchan. In many cases the name has been anglicised to Johnston(e).

MacIlwraith
From Gaelic MacGille riabhaich, 'son of the brindled lad'. Mainly a Galloway name. Other forms include MacIlriach, MacIlrick.

MacInnes
From Mac Aonghuis, 'son of Angus' (not 'son of Innes', which is not a first name). The MacInnes name was mostly found from Glen Lyon westwards.

MacIntosh

From Mac an toisich, 'son of the chief'. The chief in question was different for the Perthshire and Inverness-shire MacIntoshes, which are separate clans. The Inverness MacIntoshes of Moy were the more prominent. Also written Mackintosh. Charles Macintosh (1766–1843) patented the process of waterproofing garments. Charles Rennie Mackintosh (1868–1928) was an architect and designer whose work has had much influence. *See also* Shaw.

MacIntyre

From Mac an t-saoir, 'son of the carpenter'. The clan lands were in Glencoe, and they followed the Stewarts of Appin, although sometimes said to be a MacDonald sept. It was often anglicised to Wright. Duncan Ban MacIntyre (1724–1812) was a fine Gaelic poet.

MacIsaac *see* MacKessack.

MacIver, MacIvor

From Mac Iomhair, 'son of Ivar', from the Scandinavian name Ivarr. An Argyll clan.

MacKail

From Mac cathal, 'son of the warrior'. Cognate with MacCall. A Bute clan.

MacKay

From Mac Aoidh, 'son of Aodh', from Old Gaelic *aed*, 'fire'. The MacKay territory is around Reay in northwest Sutherland, although it is unsure when they were established there. Aodh was a popular name and MacKay or variants were also found in Kintyre and Wigtownshire. Also spelt MacKie, MacKee, and MacCoy.

MacKean

A form of MacIan. When the MacIans were driven from Ardnamurchan, early in the seventeenth century, this form, also MacKain, was taken by some who removed to Moray.

MacKechnie

From Mac Eachan, 'son of Hector'.

MacKee *see* MacGhie; MacKay.

MacKellar

From Mac Ealair, 'son of Ealar', Hilary (Latin Hilarius). An Argyll clan.

MacKenna

From Mac Cionaodha, 'son of Cionaodh', a personal name from Galloway and Arran, also spelt MacKinnie, MacKinney.

MacKenzie
From Mac Coinnich, 'son of Coinnich or Kenneth', the fair one. A numerous clan in Wester Ross and Lewis, where they dominated, but found as far south as Wigtown. Originally the z was pronounced y. Sir Alexander Mackenzie (1764–1820), explorer, discovered the Mackenzie River in Canada.

MacKercher, MacErchar
Forms of MacFarquhar. Also spelt MacCarracher.

MacKessack, MacIsaac
From Mac Iosaig, 'son of Isaac'. The name is distributed in small numbers across the central Highlands to the Moray Firth. Also spelt MacKessock.

MacKie *see* MacGhie; MacKay.

Mackie
A form of MacKay or MacKie, associated with Stirling and Galloway but now almost entirely in Aberdeenshire.

MacKillop
From Mac Fhilib, 'son of Philip'. Found in Arran, also septs of both Macdonald of Glencoe and Keppoch.

MacKinlay
From MacFhionnlaigh, 'son of Finlay'. A small clan from the southern Highlands around Balquhidder. Many removed to Ulster, and the US President MacKinley was descended from one of these.

MacKinnie, MacKinney *see* MacKenna.

MacKinnon
From Gaelic Mac Fhionnguin, 'son of Fingon', meaning fair-born. A clan with strong connections to Iona, Tiree and Kintyre.

Mackintosh *see* MacIntosh.

MacKnight *see* MacNaught.

MacKirdie, MacCurdy
From Gaelic *muir*, 'sea', and *ceartach*, 'ruler', 'sea-ruler'. An Arran and Bute clan, and an ancient name, found in pre-tenth-century annals.

MacLaughlin, MacLachlan
From MacLachlainn, 'son of Lachlann', from Gaelic Lochlann, 'Scandinavia': 'a northlander'. The clan territory was in Cowal, Argyll.

MacLaren
From Mac Labhruinn, 'son of Lawrence'. The clan was strong in Menteith and Strathearn. Also spelt MacLauren.

MacLatchie
From MacGille Eidich, 'son of the servant of Eidich', an Ayrshire and Galloway name. Also spelt MacClatchie.

MacLauren *see* **MacLaren.**

MacLeay
From Mac an leigh, 'son of the leech', or doctor. A Strathconon clan. There were also MacLeays in west Sutherland.

MacLean
From MacGille Eoin, 'son of the servant of St John'. A prominent Hebridean clan, with strongholds on Mull, Tiree and elsewhere, descended from thirteenth-century Gilleathain na Tuaidh, 'Gillean of the battle-axe'. Sorley MacLean (1911–1996) was Scotland's leading Gaelic poet of the twentieth century.

MacLehose
From MacGille Thamhais, 'son of the servant of Thomas'. A Perthshire and Stirlingshire clan.

MacLellan, MacLelland *see* **MacClelland.**

MacLeman
With MacLymont, a form of MacLamond, from MacLaomuinn, 'son of the lawman'. *See* Lamond.

MacLennan
From MacGille Fhinnein, 'son of the servant of Finnan', an Irish saint. There were MacLennans on the west coast from Galloway to Loch Broom.

MacLeod
From MacLeoid, 'son of Leod', from Scandinavian *ljotr*, 'ugly': part of a name meaning ugly wolf. A prominent clan of Skye and Lewis. Also spelt MacCloud, MacClode. John MacLeod (1876–1935), from Aberdeen, physiologist, shared the Nobel Prize for physiology and medicine, 1923.

MacLure *see* **MacClure.**

MacLurg
From Mac Luirg, 'son of the luirg', 'footman' or 'messenger'. A name found across central Scotland.

MacMartin *see* **Martin.**

MacMaster
From Mac an Mhaighstir, 'son of the master' (cleric). A sept of Clan Buchanan and also found early in Argyll, now most often found in the southwest.

MacMillan
From Mac Mhaolain or MacGille Mhaoil. Known in Argyll as Clann na Belich and so sometimes anglicised to Bell. Traced back to the Pictish Kanteai people of Moray and a prominent clan from the mid-fourteenth century, first at Knapdale, Argyll; they were forced south to Kintyre and Galloway by Campbell expansion. Kirkpatrick Macmillan (1813–78) is credited with the invention of the bicycle. Harold Macmillan (1894–1986) was a British prime minister. James Macmillan is a respected modern Scottish composer.

MacMinn
From Mac Meinne, 'son of one of the Menzies'. A Galloway name. The Menzies were known in Gaelic as Meinnearach. *See* Menzies.

MacMorran
An ancient name, chiefly connected with Galloway and Argyll, from Old Gaelic *mug*, 'slave', and *ron*, 'seal': 'the seal's slave'; perhaps from a legendary origin like the MacCodrums.

MacMunn *see* **Munn.**

MacMurdo
From Mac Murchaidh, 'son of Murdoch', from Gaelic *murchaidh*, 'sea warrior'. A name from Arran and Kintyre. *See also* Murdoch, Murchie.

MacMurray
From Gaelic Mac Muireadaigh, 'son of Muireadhach', an ancient Irish personal name. A Galloway name, not connected with Murray.

MacNab
From Mac an Aba, 'son of the abbot'; early chiefs were lay abbots of the monastery in Glendochart, heartland of the clan.

MacNair
A Wester Ross name from Mac Iain Uidhir, 'son of brown John'; in Perthshire from Mac an Oighre, 'son of the heir'; also perhaps from Mac an fhuibhir, 'son of the smith'. Sometimes anglicised to Weir.

MacNaught, MacNaughton
From Mac Neachdainn, 'son of Nechtan', 'pure one', a Pictish royal name. An Argyll clan. Also spelt MacNaghten, MacNaughten, MacKnight, MacNutt.

MacNay
From Mac Niadh, 'son of Nia', 'champion'. A name from the Argyll coast, originally from Ireland. Also spelt MacNee.

MacNeil
From Mac Niall, 'son of Neil', and claiming descent from the legendary Irish Niall of the Nine Hostages through a Niall who came to Barra in 1049. The MacNeils were hereditary bards to Clan Ranald and harpers and pipers to MacLean of Duart. Many settled in Ulster.

MacNicol
From Mac Neacail, 'son of Nicol', a form of Nicholas. Found in west Sutherland and Skye, also in the Inner Hebrides. Often changed to Nicolson. Perhaps of Scandinavian origin.

MacNulty
From mac an Ultaigh, 'son of the Ulsterman'.

MacNutt *see* MacNaught.

MacParland
A form of MacFarlane.

MacPhail
From Mac Phail, 'son of Paul'. The name is widely spread, with a MacPhail sept of Mackay in the far north, but most commonly in the Perthshire Highlands. Also spelt MacFall.

MacPhee
From Mac Dhuibhshith, from Gaelic *dhubh*, 'dark', and *sith*, 'peace', 'dark one of peace', but has also been linked to *sidh*, 'fairy'. A very old name, originating on Colonsay and found later in Lochaber. One of the names of Scotland's travelling people. Also spelt MacFee, MacHaffie, MacAfee.

MacPherson
From Mac a Phearsoin, 'son of the parson'. A prominent Badenoch clan.

MacQuade
A form of MacWatt. *See* Watt.

MacQuarie, MacQuarrie
From Mac Guaire, a personal name from Old Gaelic *gauri*, 'noble, proud'. The clan of the Isle of Ulva. Lachlan Macquarie (1761–1824) was governor of New South Wales. Also spelt MacGuire, MacWharrie.

MacQueen *see* MacSween.

MacRae
From Gaelic macrath, 'son of grace': a personal name not a patronymic, and as such originated in several different places. Mostly associated with Kintail in Wester Ross where the MacRaes were hereditary guards to the chief of MacKenzie. Also spelt MacCrae.

MacRitchie
Ritchie is a shortening of Richard (Gaelic Risdeart); an east Perthshire name. They appear to stem from one Richard MacIntosh and are linked to Clan Chattan.

MacRobert
From Mac Roibeirt, 'son of Robert'. A name from the northern fringe of the Highlands, close to the Aberdeen and Moray coasts.

MacRory
From Mac Ruaraidh, 'son of Ruaridh'. A West Highland clan, represented also in the Uists and on Islay. Also spelt MacRorie, MacRurie.

MacSporran
From Mac an Sporain, 'son of the purse'. Not a patronymic but a role name. They are said to have been hereditary purse-bearers to the Lords of the Isles. Often anglicised to Purcell.

MacSween
From MacSuibhne, 'son of Suibhne' (Sween or Sweeney, a lord of Knapdale in the early thirteenth century), an Argyll clan. The name is also rendered MacQueen and MacSweeney.

MacTaggart
From Mac an-t-sagairt, 'son of the priest'. In the Celtic church, marriage of priests was permissible, although under the influence of Queen Margaret in the twelfth century, this changed. The first record is of Ferchar or Farquhar MacTaggart in Applecross, Wester Ross, in 1215 (he became Earl of Ross), but MacTaggarts later seem to have been scattered throughout Scotland. William McTaggart (1835–1910) was a famous landscape painter.

MacTavish
From Mac Tamhais, 'son of Tammas' (a form of Thomas), an Argyll clan. The name is cognate with MacThomas, but they are separate family groups. *See also* Thomson.

MacTear
A shortened form of MacIntyre.

MacThomas
From MacThomais, 'son of Thomas'. A branch of Clan MacIntosh, descended from an illegitimate son of the seventh chief, settled in Glen Shee, Strathardle and Srathisla.

MacTurk
From Mac Tuirc, 'son of Torc', from Gaelic *torc*, 'a boar'. A Galloway name.

MacVay *see* MacBey.

MacVicar
From Mac a Bhiocar, 'son of the vicar or priest'. Unlike the MacTaggarts, they seem to have been centred in one area, Argyll, a small clan attached first to the MacNaughtons and later to the Campbells.

MacVey *see* MacBey.

MacVitie, MacVittie
Perhaps from Mac an bhiadhthaigh, 'son of the hospitaller'. A name from Galloway and Ayrshire.

MacWharrie *see* MacQuarie.

MacWhirter
A form of the name MacChruiter, from the occupation of *cruiteir*, 'harper'. The cruit was a six-stringed instrument played with a bow and the thumb. An Ayrshire and Galloway name, often anglicised to Harper.

MacWilliam
From Mac Uilleim, 'son of William'. The MacWilliams, tracing their ancestry back to Malcolm Canmore's brother, Donald Ban, were claimants to the throne for more than two hundred years. The Clan MacWilliam, however, goes back to William MacWilliam, son of the fifth chief of MacLeod. Primarily a northern clan, although forms of the name, such as MacCulliam, were current in Galloway in the seventeenth century.

M

Main
From the Scandinavian name Magnus, 'great one'. A name from the northeast, especially Nairnshire. Mann has the same derivation.

Mainland
A location name from Orkney, signifying a dweller on the Orkney mainland.

Mair
An occupational name. A mair was a sheriff's officer or other royal servant. Anglicised to Major. John Major (1469–1550) was a scholastic philosopher.

Maitland
From Norman French *Mal-talent*, or *Mautalant*, 'little wit': a nickname. Brought to Scotland from Northumberland in the thirteenth century. The Maitlands became a prominent Border family centred on Lauderdale.

Major *see* **Mair.**

Malcolm
From Gaelic *mael Coluimb*, 'follower of St Columba'. *See* MacCallum.

Mann *see* **Main.**

Manson
Shortened form of Magnusson, 'son of Magnus' (Scandinavian 'great one'). Mostly found in the north; a sept of Clan Gunn in Caithness. Sir Patrick Manson (1844–1922), born in Aberdeenshire, 'Mosquito Manson', worked on malaria with Sir Ronald Ross.

Marnoch
A location name from near Huntly in the northeast.

Marshall
An occupational name, from Old French *marechal*, Scots *marischal*, 'a farrier or blacksmith'. William Marshall (1748–1833) was a famous violinist and composer of Scottish airs.

Marr
Location name from the Aberdeenshire district of Mar. Often written Mair in former times, but *see* Mair.

Martin
A popular surname in medieval Scotland because of the veneration of St Martin of Tours, to whom St Ninian's famous church on the Isle of Whithorn, Candida Casa, had been dedicated. The Gaelic form is MacMartin, from MacGille Mhartainn, 'son of the follower of Martin'. The Macmartins of Letterfinlay, a Cameron sept, gradually changed their name to Cameron. Martin Martin (died 1719) wrote *A Description of the Western Isles of Scotland*.

Massie
Perhaps from French Masse, a pet name for Matthew.

Masson
A form of Mason, an occupational name.

Matheson
A patronymic with two possible origins. In the south, 'son of Matthew'. In the north, an anglicised form of MacMhathain, from Gaelic root words meaning 'son of the bear'.

Maule
Location name from Maule in Normandy, found in Scotland from the twelfth century.

Mavor
From Gaelic *maor*, a steward or minor official. A Speyside name originally. The real name of the playwright James Bridie (1888–1951) was Osborne Henry Mavor.

Maxwell
From Maccus, a Saxon immigrant granted lands in Tweeddale in the twelfth century. The place was Maccus *wael*, 'the well of Maccus', and from this came the family name. The Maxwells were a powerful Border clan who long feuded with the Johnstones. James Clerk Maxwell (1831–79) was a brilliant physicist, 'the father of electronics'. Gavin Maxwell (1914–69) was a writer whose book *Ring of Bright Water* was a best-seller.

Mearns
Location name from the Kincardineshire district, from *magh Eireann*, 'plain of Erin'.

Meek
Perhaps originally a devotional name, recorded from the fifteenth century, predominantly in Fife and around Perth.

Meikle
From Scots *meikle*, 'big, large': a descriptive name. Mickle is another form. Andrew Meikle (1719–1811) was the inventor of the drum threshing machine.

Meiklejohn
As with Meikle, a descriptive name but with the most common forename also attached. It originates on the north side of the Firth of Forth.

Meldrum
Location name from Aberdeenshire, from Gaelic *meall druim*, 'mountain ridge'.

Melville, Melvil
Location name brought from Malleville in Normandy, recorded first in the twelfth century. The de Mallevilles settled in Lothian and Fife. Variants of the name include Melvin and Melven. Andrew Melville (1545–c.1622) was a leading Protestant Reformer.

Mennie
Location name from inland Aberdeenshire, from Mennie, near Banchory.

Menzies
Location name from a Norman manor, Meyners, brought to Scotland in the twelfth century. The English form is Manners.

Michie
From a shortened form of Michael, a name originating in the Strathdon area of Aberdeenshire, first recorded in 1570.

Mickle *see* Meikle.

Millar, Miller
Occupation name; Millar is the typically Scottish form, although Miller is more often found. There was a Millar sept of Clan MacFarlane. Hugh Miller (1802–56), born in Cromarty, was a geologist, writer and religious reformer; William Miller (1810–72) wrote 'Wee Willie Winkie'.

Miln, Milne
From Middle English and Scots *mylne*, 'a mill': 'one who dwells by the mill'. Chiefly found in Aberdeenshire and Angus. Also spelt Mylne.

Mitchell
From the Hebrew name Michael ('who is like God'); but can also be from Middle English and Scots *mickle*, 'big'. In the northeast the Mitchells were a sept of Clan Innes.

Moar
A Shetland name, perhaps a form of Moir, although it may be from an old location name, Mowir.

Moffat
Location name from the Border town, first noted in 1232, from Gaelic *magh fada*, 'long plain'. The Moffats were among the numerous small Border clans who flourished until the Union of the Crowns in 1603. James Moffat (1870–1944) produced a famous translation of the Bible into modern English.

Moir
From Gaelic *mor*, 'large': a descriptive name, Chiefly found in the Aberdeen area. Also spelt More, which is the form more common in the north. *See also* Moar.

Moncreiffe
Location name from lands in Dunbarny parish, Perthshire, recorded as Moncriefe from the thirteenth century. From Gaelic *monadh craoibh*, 'wooded hill'. Sir Iain Moncrieffe of that Ilk (1919–85) was a well-known authority on genealogy.

Monro, Monroe *see* **Munro.**

Monteith
Location name from Menteith in Perthshire.

Moodie
Perhaps from Old English *modig*, 'brave'. Recorded from the fourteenth century. Mudie is another form of the name.

More *see* **Moir.**

Morrice
More common in the northeast than the Morris form.

Morris
The baptismal name Maurice was brought by the Normans (from Latin *Maurus*, 'a Moor'). Tom Morris (1821–1908), born in St Andrews, was one of the founders of modern golf.

Morrison, Morison
In the Lowlands, from 'son of Morris or Maurice'. The Lewis Morrisons came from Ireland as O'Morrison, from Gaelic *muirgheas*, 'sea bravery'. They dropped the O prefix. They were a bardic clan, their chief the hereditary judge of the island. Robert Morison (1620–83), born in Aberdeen, became the first professor of botany at Oxford.

Morton
A location name from Dumfriesshire and also Fife, from Scots *muirton*, 'farm by the moor'. Alan Morton (1893–1971), 'the wee blue deevil', was a celebrated international footballer.

Mowat, Mouat
From Norman French *mont hault*, 'high mount', found now mostly in the north, although the Normans of this name originally settled in Angus.

Moultrie
The earliest form is Multreve, 1292; it is the name of an estate now occupied by the Register House in Edinburgh.

Muckersie
Location name from Perthshire, from Gaelic *muc*, 'sow', and Scandinavian *kerss*, 'low-lying river bank'.

Mudie *see* Moodie.

Muir
From Scots *muir*, 'a moor': 'dweller on the moorland'. John Muir (1838–1914), born in Dunbar, emigrated to the USA and became the founder of the environmental movement. Edwin Muir (1887–1959), born in Orkney, was a major Scottish poet.

Muirden
Location name from near Turriff, Aberdeenshire, Scots *muir dean*, 'valley in the moor'.

Muirhead
Another of the numerous Muir-names, from the Southern Uplands in this case, a location name from Lanarkshire.

Munn
St Munn is a form of the name of St Fintan (died 635), whose name is preserved in this form in Kilmun, Argyll. The reduced form of MacMunn is a name from the Cowal district.

Munro
Perhaps from Gaelic *monadh ruadh*, 'red mountain'; an Easter Ross clan. Alternatively derived from Gaelic *Rothach*, 'man of Ro', from a supposed origin by the River Roe in Ireland. Also spelt Monro, Monroe. Neil Munro (1864–1930), born in Inveraray, was a novelist and author of the Para Handy tales. James Monroe, fifth president of the USA, was descended from the Munros.

Murchie, Murchison
English forms of Gaelic *murchaidh*, 'sea warrior', and 'son of Murchaidh' (Murdo or Murdoch). *See* MacMurdo. Sir Roderick Murchison (1792–1871), born near Muir of Ord, was a pioneering geologist.

Murdoch
See Murchie. William Murdoch (1754–1839) invented gas lighting and was proclaimed a deity by the then shah of Persia, who thought him a reincarnation of Marduk, god of light.

Murieson
An Aberdeenshire name, perhaps a form of Morrison.

Murray
Location name from the province of Moray, from Old Gaelic *mur*, 'sea', and ending *-aibh*, 'by the sea'. The first was Freskin de Moravia, an immigrant lord of the twelfth century. His grandson was the ancestor of the Murrays of Tullibardine, the great Atholl clan. Sir James Murray (1837–1915), born in Denholm, was the founding editor of the Oxford English Dictionary.

Mushet
Scots form of Norman Montfiquet, a location name from Normandy, first recorded in 1165. William de Montefixo was a signatory of the Declaration of Arbroath, 1320.

Mutch
Recorded in Stirling from 1520, but nothing is known of the origins of the name.

Mylne *see* Miln.

N

Nairn
Location name from the town. First recorded as de Narryn in 1361.

Naismith *see* Nasmyth.

Napier
Occupational name, from the official in charge of cloths and linens at the royal court. John Napier of Merchiston (1550–1617) invented logarithms.

Nasmyth
Occupational name, meaning knife-smith: knife-maker or grinder. Alexander Nasmyth (1758–1840) was a successful painter, his son James (1808–90) an inventive mechanical engineer. Also spelt Naismith.

Naughtie
Location name from Nochty in Strathdon, Aberdeenshire, recorded from 1450. Perhaps from Gaelic *nochdaidh*, 'desolate'.

Neil, Neill, Neilson
From Gaelic Niall, which became Old Norse Njal. In Norman French it was Nesle, which was thought to mean black and gave rise to the name Nigel, from Latin *niger*, 'black'. There were Neilsons on Bute, a sept of the Stewarts, and also in Sutherland, a sept of Clan MacKay. A. S. Neill (1883–1973) was an influential educationalist.

Newall
A Scots form of both Noel and Neville (Old French *neuville*, 'new place'); mostly found in the southwest.

Nicol, Nicholl
A shortened form of Nicholas, a name brought by the Normans, from Greek, 'victory of the people'. *See* MacNicol.

Nish
From Gaelic *nis*, 'a promontory': 'dweller on the ness'. A name from the southwest.

Niven
From Gaelic *naomhain*, 'little saint'. A devotional name found in Galloway and Ayrshire.

Noble
A name first recorded in Lothian in the twelfth century but now associated more with the area around Inverness, where it was a sept name of Clan MacIntosh, and Easter Ross around Muir of Ord.

Norie, Norrie
From Scandinavian *Norge*, 'Norway', as a name in the northern area. May also be from Norrie, a pet form of Norman, in the south.

Norquoy
From Scandinavian *nord kvi*, 'north fold'. An Orkney location name.

O

Oag, Ogg
From Gaelic *og*, 'young': a descriptive name to designate a boy whose father, of the same name, was either still alive or well known.

Ochiltree
Location name from West Lothian, from Old British *ocel tre*, 'high house'.

Ogilvie
Location name from near Glamis in Angus, from Old British *ocel*, 'high', and *fa*, 'plain' (or perhaps Gaelic *bheinn*, 'mountain'). St John Ogilvie (1579–1615) was a Catholic martyr, hanged in Glasgow.

Ogston
Location name from Hogeston in Moray, from 'hogs toun', 'sheep farm'.

Oliphant
A Norman name, originally Olifard, a form of Oliver, which was altered to Oliphant (the coat of arms showed an elephant). Carolina Oliphant, Lady Nairne (1766–1845), wrote many well-known songs, including 'Will Ye No' Come Back Again?'

Oliver
A Norman name, cognate with Oliphant, from Olivier, 'olive bearer'. In Shetland the name Olaf has been merged into Oliver.

Ord
Location name from Banffshire, from Gaelic *ord*, 'a rounded height'.

Ordie
From a diminutive form of Ord.

Orr
A Renfrewshire and Argyll name, perhaps cognate with Ure. A sept of Clan Campbell.

P

Paden *see* **Peden.**

Park
Location name from Park, in Renfrewshire, written originally as de Parco. Mungo Park (1771–1806), born in Foulshiels in the Borders, was an explorer of Africa.

Pate *see* **Peat.**

Paterson
Patronymic: 'son of Patrick or Pat'. Also spelt Patterson. William Paterson (1658–1719), born near Lochmaben, founded the Bank of England.

Patey *see* **Peat.**

Patience
Localised to certain districts including the Black Isle.

Paton, Patton
From a pet form of Patrick, Pat. This was a common baptismal name until the Reformation (sixteenth century). Once common in the southwest, now found more in the east.

Patterson *see* **Paterson.**

Patton *see* **Paton.**

Pattullo
Location name from Fife and Glenfarg. In former times also spelt Pittillo, and probably of Pictish origin like other Pit- names.

Peat
Diminutive form of Peter. Other forms include Pate and Patey. From Greek *petros*, 'a rock', and the name of the leader of the Apostles. All these forms are found on the central east coast.

Peddie
Another diminutive of Peter. *See* Peat.

Peden
A diminutive form of Patrick. Also spelt Paden. Alexander Peden (*c.*1626–86) was a controversial figure among the Protestant reformers.

Pendreich, Pendreigh
Shortened forms of Pittendreigh; a location name from near Bridge of Allan. Pittendrigh MacGillivray (1856–1938) was well known as a Scottish sculptor and poet.

Petrie
May be a diminutive either of Peter or of Patrick; once often written Patre. A name chiefly from the Aberdeen area.

Pettigrew
A Lanarkshire name, its origins perhaps from Scots *petty*, 'small', and 'grove', meaning the owner or tenant of a wood or orchard.

Pinkerton
Location name from East Lothian. Allan Pinkerton (1819–84), founder of the American detective agency, was born in Glasgow.

Pirie
A diminutive of Peter, through the French form Pierre. *See also* Peat.

Pitcairn
Location name of Pictish origin from Pitcairn in Fife. Archibald Pitcairne (1652–1713), doctor and satirist, reformed medical teaching in Edinburgh. Pitcairn Island was named after Robert Pitcairn RN (1767).

Pittillo *see* **Pattullo.**

Playfair
Perhaps derived from old Scots *playfeire*, 'playfellow'. William Henry
Playfair (1789–1857) was the architect of many notable buildings includ-
ing the National Gallery and the National Monument in Edinburgh.

Pollock
Location name from Renfrewshire, meaning 'little pool'. In the USA the
name became Polk. President Polk was of descent from the Scots Pollocks.

Polson
'Son of Paul'. A name from Orkney and the north. The Shetland form is
Poleson.

Porteous
A name from the southwest, perhaps derived from 'port-house'. John
Porteous (died 1736), captain of the Edinburgh guard, was hanged by the
city mob.

Pottinger
From French *potager*, 'a gardener'. A name from the Northern Isles.

Pow
From Scots *pow*, 'head', perhaps originally a descriptive name or nickname.

Powrie
Location name from Errol on Tayside.

Pringle
Originally Hoppringle, a location name from Roxburghshire and still a
Border name. Sir John Pringle (1707–82) was a pioneer of military
medicine.

Proudfoot
Originally a nickname for one with a haughty gait. Most common in the
southwest.

Purcell *see* **MacSporran.**

Pyper
Occupational name for a piper and, although not common, is scattered all
round the edges of the Highlands up to Wick.

R

Rae
From Gaelic *rath*, 'grace'. John Rae (1813–93), born in Stromness, was an Arctic explorer.

Raeburn
A form of Ryburn, a location name from near Dunlop in Ayrshire. Sir Henry Raeburn (1756–1823) was one of Scotland's great portrait painters.

Rainey, Rainy *see* **Rennie.**

Ramsay
A location name from Ramsay, meaning 'ram's island', in Huntingdonshire, England, whose lord received lands in Scotland in the twelfth century. Allan Ramsay (*c*.1685–1758), a poet, wrote 'The Gentle Shepherd'; his son, Allan (1713–84), was a famous portrait painter.

Rankin, Rankine
From a pet form of Randolph, with -kin added. An Ayrshire name.

Rattray
Location name from Rattray in Perthshire, from Old Gaelic *rath tref*, 'mound dwelling'.

Ratter
Location name from Caithness, now largely a Shetland name.

Redpath
Location name from Redpath in Berwickshire. James Redpath (1833–91), born in Berwick, became a prominent American political journalist; Jean Redpath (born 1937) is a well-known singer of Burns' songs.

Reid
From Old English and Scots *red* (pronounced reed), a descriptive colour name. Also the English version of Gaelic MacRuaraidh, MacRory, from Gaelic *ruadh*, 'red'. Sir William Reid (1791–1858), born in Kinglassie, Fife, was a colonial governor and an expert on winds and storms.

Rendall
An Orkney name, perhaps from Randolph but more likely a location name from the parish of Rendall, from Scandinavian *renna dal*, 'valley of running water'. Robert Rendall, born in Kirkwall, was a regional poet of distinction.

Rennie
From Norman French Reynaud, Reynold (Scandinavian Ragnhild, 'counsel-power'). John Rennie (1761–1821) was a leading civil engineer. Also spelt Rainy, Rainey.

Renwick
Location name from Renwick in Cumberland, formerly 'ravens' wick' or 'farm'.

Rettie
Location name from Rettie or Reattie in Banffshire.

Rhind
Location name from Rhynd in Perthshire, from Gaelic *roin*, 'point of land'. Alexander Rhind (1833–63)' born in Wick, was an archaeologist specialising in ancient Egypt.

Riach
From Gaelic *riabhach*, 'brindled, greyish', a descriptive name. Also spelt Rioch.

Riddel, Riddell
From two sources, the Ridels of Gascony, or the de Rydales of Ryedale in North Yorkshire, a Norman family. Both are recorded from the twelfth century. Originally from the Borders, it is now a northeast name.

Ritchie
From Richie, a pet form of Richard. Sometimes shortened from MacRitchie. William Ritchie founded the *Scotsman* newspaper, 1817.

Robb
A shortened form of Robert.

Roberton
Location name from Lanarkshire, 'Robert's farmstead'. Sir Hugh Roberton was a famous conductor of the Glasgow Orpheus Choir.

Roberts
Patronymic: 'son of Robert'. Less common in Scotland than Robertson.

David Roberts (1796–1864), born in Edinburgh, became famous as a painter of Middle Eastern scenes.

Robertson
Son of Robert. In Gaelic the Clan Donnchaidh or Duncan, *c.*1500 it took the name of the first chief. Jeannie Robertson (1908–75), born in Aberdeen, was perhaps the last of the great true Scottish folksingers.

Roddie
A doubly shortened form of Roderick. Another form is Roddick.

Rollo
From the personal name Rudolf or Rolf. A northeast name. The form Rollock is now very rare.

Ronaldson
Son of Ronald or Ranald, from Scandinavian Rognvaldr, 'ruler of counsel'.

Rose
Cognate with Ross, a name long linked with Kilravock in Nairnshire

Rosie *see* **Rossie.**

Ross
From Gaelic *ros*, 'a promontory'; 'the dwellers on the promontory'. The clan Ross territory is in Easter Ross, but there were also Rosses in Galloway. Sir James Clark Ross (1800–62), polar explorer, discovered the sea named after him; Sir Ronald Ross (1857–1932) found the cure for malaria.

Rossie, Rosie
Location name from Fife, of the same derivation as Ross.

Rothnie
Location name from Premnay parish, Aberdeenshire.

Rough
A form of Rock, from the Norman name de la Roche, or from St Roch. A Fife name.

Rougvie
A Perthshire and Fife name, origin uncertain, perhaps related to Gaelic *ruicean*, 'pimple'.

Row
From Gaelic *ruadh*, 'red': 'the red-haired or red-faced one'.

Roy
From Gaelic *ruadh*, 'red': 'the red-haired or red-faced one'. *See also* Reid.

Runciman
From Scots *rouncie*, 'a saddle horse': 'groom or ostler'. Found in Aberdeenshire and Kinross but chiefly in the Borders. A shortened form is Runcie.

Russell
From old French *rous*, 'red-haired'. There were Russell septs of Clans Buchanan and Cumming, but it is chiefly a Lowland name.

Rutherford
A location name from Maxton, Roxburghshire, Old English *hrythera*, 'ford', 'ford of the horned cattle'. A reiving clan. Also spelt Rutherfurd. Samuel Rutherford (*c.*1600–1661), born near Jedburgh, was an eminent but controversial theologian; Lord Rutherford (1871–1937), born in New Zealand of Scottish parents, was a founder of nuclear physics (Nobel Prize-winner 1908).

Ruthven
A location name from Angus, from Gaelic *ruadh abhainn*, 'red river'. Of Scandinavian descent, the family became lords of Ruthven and earls of Gowrie. The name was proscribed in 1600 but reinstated in 1641.

Ryrie
Probably from Gaelic Ruaraidh, Roderick. MacRyrie was a sept of MacDonald but is current now without the Mac.

S

Sanderson
'Son of Sanders', a common diminutive form of Alexander, found in various areas from the fifteenth century onwards.

Sandison
'Son of Sandy', a common diminutive form of Alexander. Chiefly a Moray and Shetland name.

Sangster
From Scots *sangster*, 'singer'; an occupational name for a chorister or precentor, found in the northeast.

Scarth
A location name from Scarth in the Orkney parish of Firth, perhaps from Scandinavian *skorf*, 'cormorant'.

Sclater, Slater
Occupational name for a slater or tiler. By the time it moved to Orkney and Shetland, the occupational connection was lost.

Scobie
Location name from Scobie in Perthshire.

Scollay
Location name from Skaill in Sandwick. An Orkney and Shetland name.

Scorgie
Perhaps a form of Scroggie. A northeast name.

Scott
Scot originally meant a Gael, but the surname arose in the Border area where it meant someone from Scotland. The Scotts were among the most prominent Border clans. Michael Scott (*c*.1170–1230), scholar, has left a reputation for wizardry in many places; Sir Walter Scott (1771–1832) remains Scotland's greatest novelist.

Scougal
Location name from Scougal, now Seacliffe, East Lothian. From Scandinavian *skogr*, 'wood', and *hale*, 'hole or nook'.

Scoular
From Scots, 'keeper of a school'. Chiefly from Lanarkshire.

Scroggie
Location name from Scroggie in Perthshire but also known in Aberdeenshire. From Scots *scroggie*, 'thorny, rough'.

Scrymgeour
From Middle English and Scots *scrimscher* or *skrymsher*, 'a swordsman' or 'fencer'. The Scrymgeours were hereditary standard-bearers to Scottish kings and supporters of Wallace in the independence struggle. Originally based in Fife, but long associated with Dundee.

Seaton *see* Seton.

Seatter
Location name from Setter, by Stromness, Orkney. From Scandinavian *saetr*, 'farm'.

Selkirk
Location name from the Border town, from Old English *sele*, 'house', and *kirk*, 'church'. Alexander Selkirk (1676–1721), born in Largo, Fife, was the model for Defoe's Robinson Crusoe.

Sellar
Probably from Middle English *seler*, 'saddler'.

Semple, Sempill
Perhaps from the French location name St Pol. The earliest version is de Sempill, around 1280.

Seton, Seaton
Location name from Sai in Normandy, first found in Scotland *c.*1150. The Setons became a prominent family, closely associated with the Crown.

Shand
A name from the western side of Aberdeenshire, around Turiff and Fyvie. Possibly French in origin. Jimmy Shand was a leading exponent of Scottish dance music in the twentieth century.

Shankly
A form of Shankilaw, 'Shank's hill', a Lanarkshire name. Bill Shankly (1913–81) was an exceptional football manager.

Sharp, Shairp
A nickname. Archbishop Sharp of St Andrews was murdered in 1679. William Sharp (1855–1905), born in Paisley, wrote Celtic romances under the name of Fiona MacLeod.

Shaw
In the south, from Old English *sceaga*, 'wood': 'dweller by the wood'; in the Highlands the Shaws descend from a branch of the Clan MacIntosh, founded by Sithic (Gaelic 'wolf-like'), anglicised to Shaw. Norman Shaw (1831–1912), born in Edinburgh, was a prolific architect and town planner.

Shearer
An occupational name, 'sheep-shearer'.

Shiach
From Old Gaelic *sithech*, 'wolf'. An Aberdeenshire and Moray name, cognate with Shaw.

Shields
From Old English *schele*, 'a shieling': 'dweller in, or builder of, the shieling'. A Border name.

Sibbald
From the Old English name Saebeald, meaning 'sea bold'; primarily a Fife name. Sir Robert Sibbald (1641–1722), born in Edinburgh, was a distinguished naturalist and doctor.

Sim, Sims
Shortened forms of Simon. *See* Simpson.

Simpson
Son of Simon, shortened to Sim (originally Hebrew *shim'on*, 'listener'). Sir James Young Simpson (1811–70), born in Bathgate, was a pioneer of gynaecology and anaesthetics.

Sinclair
From Norman-French St-Clair, a family who became barons of Roslin, near Edinburgh, then earls of Caithness. The name was then adopted by their tenants. Sir John Sinclair (1754–1835), born in Thurso, was a leading improver of agricultural methods.

Skene
A location name from Aberdeenshire, from Gaelic *sceathain*, 'bush'. William Forbes Skene (1809–92), born in Inverie, was a leading historian of early Scotland.

Skinner
An occupational name for a flayer of animal hides. Most common in the Moray Firth area. James Scott Skinner (1843–1927), born in Banchory, was a celebrated violinist and composer.

Slater *see* Sclater.

Slessor
Perhaps a Dutch immigrant name, found in Aberdeen and Angus. Mary Slessor (1848–1915), born in Aberdeen, was a famous missionary in Calabar, Nigeria.

Sloan
From Irish O' Sluaghain, 'son of the war leader'. A name from the southwest.

Smail, Small
A descriptive name; Smail is the Scots form.

Smellie, Smillie
Possibly derived from Smalley, a location name in Derbyshire, England. A name from Glasgow and Lanarkshire. Also spelt Smyllie, Smiley.

Smith
The single most common name in Scotland. An occupational name, often an anglicisation of Gaelic MacGobha (*see* Gow, MacGowan). Adam Smith (1723–90), born in Kirkcaldy, economist, was one of the founders of economic life today; Sir William Smith (1846–94), born in Keig, Aberdeenshire, founded the Boys' Brigade.

Smollett
A Dumbartonshire name, the etymology of which has been tentatively linked with the name Samuel. Tobias Smollett (1721–71), the novelist, was born in Dumbartonshire.

Smyllie *see* Smellie.

Soutar, Souter
An occupational name from Scots *soutar*, 'shoemaker'. The name is widely distributed in the Lowland areas. William Soutar (1898–1943), born in Perth, was a distinguished Scots poet.

Spankie
A descriptive name from Angus and Kincardineshire, from Scots *spankie*, 'spirited, sprightly'.

Spens, Spence
From Middle English and Scots *spence*, 'provisioner': 'in charge of the larder'. Catherine Spence (1825–1910), born of Scottish immigrant parents, was a pioneer Australian feminist.

Spiers
Probably from 'spier' or 'lookout' (Old French *espier*).

Spottiswoode
A location name from lands in Berwickshire. John Spottiswoode (1565–1639), archbishop of St Andrews, crowned Charles II in Edinburgh, 1633.

Sprott, Sproat
From an Old English name, Sprot. First recorded in 1262.

Steel, Steele
A location name from several places in Ayrshire and the Borders. The Berwickshire parish of Ladykirk was once Steill.

Stein
A shortened form of Steven or Stevenson, from Fife and the Lothians. Jock Stein (1922–85) was another of Scotland's notable football managers.

Stephen, Steven
A name brought by the Normans, commemorating the first Christian martyr. Steven is more common, but Stephen is found in the northeast and north.

Stevenson
Son of Steven. Robert Louis Stevenson (1850–94), born in Edinburgh, novelist and poet, died on Samoa.

Stewart
From Old English *stigweard*, 'keeper of a great house'; extended in Scotland to mean steward of the royal household, the king's chief administrator. The family name of Scottish, later British, kings from Robert II (1371) to Queen Anne (died 1714). They came from Dol in Brittany in the early twelfth century. Stewart territories were established in Appin, Atholl, Bute and Galloway, effectively becoming separate clans with one name. Also spelt Stuart since the sixteenth century. *See also* MacGregor.

Still
A northeast name, possibly a form of Steel.

Stirling
Location name from the town, although Stirlings are found quite widely from an early date. Patrick Stirling (1820–95), born in Kilmarnock, was a leading locomotive designer.

Stitt
A name from the southwest.

Stott
Possibly a nickname from *stot*, 'a heifer', but more probably a form of Stout, itself from Old English *steorte*, 'a tongue of land': a location rather than a descriptive name.

Strachan, Strahan
Location name from Strachan in Kincardineshire, from Gaelic *strath eithin*, 'valley of the river'.

Strang
Probably from Old French *estrange*, 'foreign', rather than Scots *strang*, 'strong'. An east coast immigration name, first found as le Estraunge in 1255.

Striven
A Bute name, from Gaelic Strath Fionn, 'the white strath'.

Stronach
From Gaelic *sron*, 'nose'; a nickname, either 'big-nose' or 'nosy'; or possibly a location name from one who lives on the nose or point. Chiefly an Aberdeenshire name.

Struthers
A location name from Northumberland, 'dweller by the marshy land'.

Stuart *see* **Stewart.**

Sutherland
Location name from the county, from Scandinavian *sudr land*, 'land to the south'. The lands of the Clan Sutherland were to the east side.

Suttie
A Perth name, of uncertain origin.

Swan
A form of Swain, from the Scandinavian personal name Swein. Most common in the southeast. Annie S. Swan (1859–1943), born in Berwickshire, was an immensely successful popular novelist.

Swanson
Son of Swain (*see* Swan); a Caithness name.

Syme *see* **Simpson.**

Symington
Location name from Lanarkshire, from 'Symon's town'. William Symington (1763–1831), born in Leadhills, inventor, was designer of the first practical steam-powered craft.

T

Taggart *see* **MacTaggart.**

Tait
From Scandinavian *teitr*, 'cheerful, gay' (*see* Jolly). A Border clan, allied to the Kerrs. Archibald Campbell Tait (1811–82), born in Edinburgh, was the first Scot to become archbishop of Canterbury (1869).

Tamson
'Son of Tam', another Scots form of Thomson.

Tannahill
Location name from Ayrshire. Robert Tannahill (1774–1810), born in Paisley, was a gifted poet and songwriter.

Tarrel
Location name from the area on Tarbat Ness, Ross-shire, from Gaelic *tar al*, 'above the cliff'.

Tassie
Probably from Old French *taisson*, 'badger', rather than Scots *tassie*, 'a cup'. Found as Tassin in 1296. A name from the Glasgow area.

Tawse
A form of Gaelic Tamhas, Thomas, found mostly in Aberdeenshire; not related to Scots *tawse*, 'strap'.

Taylor, Taylour
Occupational name from 'tailor', well distributed through the country from the thirteenth century.

Telfer, Telford
From Norman French *taille-fer*, 'cut iron', perhaps a trade name, and found in central and southern Scotland. Telford is the same name with an accreted -d. Thomas Telford (1757–1834), born in Langholm, was a celebrated civil engineer.

Tennant, Tennent
'One who holds land on a lease'. First recorded in Linlithgow, 1296, but
more often found in Glasgow and Stirling.

Thain
Perhaps from Middle English and Scots *thegn*, 'a nobleman'. A name from
upland Banffshire.

Thin
A descriptive name or nickname, found in Edinburgh and on the east
coast.

Thom
A shortened form of Thomas.

Thomson
'Son of Thomas'. One of the most common names in Scotland, often as
an anglicised form of MacTavish or MacCombie. Thomas comes via
Anglo-Norman from Hebrew *to-am*, 'twin'. James Thomson (1700–
1748), born in Kelso, was the poet of *The Seasons*; Robert William
Thomson (1822–73), born in Stonehaven, was a versatile engineer who
patented the fountain pen.

Thorburn
From Old English Thurbrand, related to Scandinavian Thor, god of
thunder: 'sword of Thor'. Found as Thorburn from the sixteenth century.
A name from Lothian and Dumfries. Archibald Thorburn (1860–1935),
born in Lasswade, was a gifted bird artist.

Tod, Todd
From Old English and Scots *tod*, 'fox', a nickname. The extra -d was
added in the eighteenth century, mostly on the east coast; Tod remains on
the west.

Tolmie
A form of Gaelic Talvaich, a Hebridean clan, but the name is also found
in Inverness and Easter Ross.

Torrance
Location name from Torrance in Stirlingshire and Lanarkshire, from
either Gaelic *torr*, 'a craggy height', or Old French *tour*, 'tower'.

Tosh
A shortened form of MacIntosh.

Toshack
From Gaelic *toiseach*, 'chief', a translation of 'thane'. The Toshacks resided in Glentilt, where Finlay of that name was referred to as Thane of Glentilt in the early sixteenth century.

Tough
From Gaelic *tulach*, 'a hill'; a location name from near Alford, Aberdeenshire. Also written Touch.

Traill
Origin of this name is uncertain; first recorded in the fourteenth century at Blebo in Fife, and the same family established itself in Orkney.

Tranter
Occupational name, from Middle English and Scots, 'a carrier or hawker'. Nigel Tranter is a widely read historical novelist.

Troup
Location name from Troup in Banffshire; its origin is uncertain.

Trumble *see* **Turnbull.**

Tuach
A Ross-shire name, perhaps from Gaelic *tulach*, 'hill' (*see* Tough).

Tudhope
Location name from near Jedburgh, 'Tuda's hollow or enclosure'.

Tulloch
Location name perhaps from the estate of Tulloch, by Dingwall, from Gaelic *tulach*, 'hill', although well spread from Orkney to Aberdeen by the fourteenth century.

Turnbull
Probably from Old English *trumbald*, 'strong and bold', and spelt Trumble or Turnbull from the fourteenth century. A reiving Border clan.

Twatt
Location name from both Orkney and Shetland, from Scandinavian *thveit*, 'place' (English 'thwaite').

Tweedie
Location name from Tweedside. A sept of Clan Fraser, from its Frisell Border form.

u

Ure
A form of Ivor, probably shortened from MacUre. Andrew Ure (1778–1857), born in Glasgow, was author of *A Dictionary of Chemistry*.

Urie
From Gaelic *iubharach*, 'abounding in yew trees': 'dweller among the yews'.

Urquhart
Location name from Inverness-shire, perhaps originally from Orchard. The Urquharts were hereditary sheriffs of Cromarty. Sir Thomas Urquhart (*c.*1611–1660), born in Cromarty, author and translator, is famous for his English version of Rabelais.

Usher
From Middle English *uschere*, 'a doorkeeper'. Once interchangeable with Durward.

V

Vass
From Old French *vaux*, 'valleys'. A Norman-English name, settlers in Lothian, but Vass is now found largely in Aberdeen and Ross-shire.

Veitch
Perhaps from Latin *vacca*, 'cow', French *vache*. the oldest form of the name is de Vacca or Vache; perhaps from Old English Ucca, a personal name. A name associated with Tweeddale.

W

Waddell
Location name from Wedale, now Stow, Midlothian, still primarily an Edinburgh and Lothian name.

Waldie
Shortened form of Waldeve, from Old English Waltheof, a personal name; long established in the Kelso area.

Walker
An occupational name, from the process of waulking cloth, equivalent to the English name Fuller. First recorded in 1324. The Gaelic form was MacFhucadair, 'son of the fuller', but does not survive.

Wallace
Cognate with Welsh and Walsh; a name from Strathclyde that recalls the original language of the region, akin to Welsh rather than Gaelic. Sir William Wallace (c.1274–1305) was one of Scotland's greatest patriots and heroes.

Walls
An Orkney name, from the island of Walls.

Walsh, Welsh
From Middle English *walsche*, meaning 'a Welshman' or 'foreigner'.

Wardlaw
From Middle English and Scots *ward*, 'guard, lookout', and *law*, 'hill'. There is a Wardlaw Hill near Beauly, but the name is associated with Fife and Edinburgh. Bishop Henry Wardlaw (died 1440) was a founder of St Andrews University.

Wardie
From Old English *worthi*, 'farm'; 'farm-dweller'.

Wardrop, Wardrope
Occupational name, from keeper of the royal or nobleman's wardrobe. This entailed caring for furniture, etc, as well as garments.

Wares
A location name from Wares in Caithness.

Wark
A location name from Wark, Northumberland; from Middle English *wark*, 'a work' or 'building'.

Waters, Watters
Patronymics; forms of 'Walter's son'. Also Waterson.

Waterston, Waterstone
Location name, 'Walter's place', from several locations in the south. The Scottish physicist John James Waterston (1811–83) anticipated important theories in kinetics and thermodynamics.

Watret
A Dumfriesshire name, from Whutterick, a form of MacKettrick.

Watson
'Son of Wat or Watt'. *See* Watt. There were Watsons in the southwest as well as the northeast. There is a possible Gaelic derivation from Mac Bhaididh, although this would give MacWattie.

Watt
From the Anglo-Saxon personal name Walter, shortened. Most frequent in the northeast. James Watt (1736–1819) developed an efficient steam engine; Sir Robert Watson-Watt (1892–1973) played a key part in the development of radar.

Watters *see* **Waters.**

Wauchope
Location name from the Langholm area, although it is chiefly associated with Peebles and Roxburghshire. From Old English *walc*, 'stranger', and *hop*, 'hollow place': 'the den of strangers'.

Waugh
A shortened form of Wauchope, also associated with Peebles and Roxburgh.

Webster
Occupational name from Scots *webster*, 'weaver'.

Wedderburn
Location name from Berwickshire, 'burn of the wether or sheep', first recorded in the late thirteenth century.

Weir
From Norman Vere, a location name from Normandy, from Scandinavian *ver*, 'a stance or station'. A Lanarkshire name. The unrelated Gaelic name MacNair was anglicised to Weir.

Welsh
A name from the southwest, cognate with Walsh.

Wemyss
A location name from Wemyss in Fife, from Gaelic *uamh*, 'cave'.

White *see* **Whyte.**

Whitelaw
Location name from the lands of Whitelaw ('white hill'), Morebattle.

Whyte, White
From Old English *hwyt*, 'pale': a nickname, but often an anglicised version of Gaelic MacGille Bhain, 'son of the fair youth or servant'. The name was also chosen by proscribed Lamonds and MacGregors.

Wilkie
A pet form of William, from Midlothian. Sir David Wilkie (1785–1841), born in Cults, was a distinguished painter particularly known for his genre scenes.

Will
A shortened form of William, a northeast name.

Williamson
In the Middle Ages, William was one of the most common male baptismal names, hence the many versions of it that now exist. Many MacWilliams in the Highlands, septs to MacKay and Gunn, became Williamson. *See* MacWilliam.

Willox
From Willoc, 'little William', a northeast name.

Wilson
A form of Williamson, most frequent in the central area and one of the top five surnames. Also a sept name to Clans Gunn in the north and Innes in the northeast. Charles Wilson (1869–1959), born in Glencorse, made major contributions to nuclear physics and shared the Nobel Prize for physics in 1927.

Wiseman
From Middle English and Scots *wyse*, 'learned, sagacious'. A Moray name, also found in Shetland.

Wishart
From Norman French *guischard*, 'prudent'; an east coast name from Aberdeen to Edinburgh. George Wishart (1513–46), Protestant reformer, was burned at St Andrews.

Witherspoon, Wotherspoon
Partly from Middle English and Scots *wether*, 'sheep', although the source of the ending is uncertain. A name found along the lowland areas of the east coast.

Wood
'Dweller in or by the wood'. Sir Andrew Wood (*c.*1455–1539) was the first notable Scottish naval commander.

Wordie
Recorded from the sixteenth century onwards, probably from the same source as Wardie.

Work
Location name from the parish of St Ola in Orkney.

Wotherspoon *see* Witherspoon.

Wright
In the south, from Old English *wryhta*, 'woodworker', a trade name. *See* MacIntyre.

Wylie
From a pet form of William, Willie, found in numerous places south of the Highland line.

Wyness
A northeast name. An older form, Wynhouse, suggests a possible occupational name.

Y

Yarrow
A location name from the river in the Southern Uplands.

Young
From Old English *geong*, 'young', used to differentiate father and son of the same first name. *See also* Auld, Oag. Andrew Young (1855–1971), born in Elgin, was a gifted poet.

Youngson
'Son of Young', a name associated almost entirely with Aberdeenshire.

Younie
Probably from the Gaelic name Adhamnan; a Moray name.

Yuill
Perhaps from Yule, meaning one born at Yuletide. Found in Fife and Aberdeenshire, but mainly associated with Stirlingshire, where the Yuills were a sept of Clan Buchanan.